I Think I'll Major in Education

B.G. Tate

authorHOUSE®

AuthorHouse™
1663 Liberty Drive
Bloomington, IN 47403
www.authorhouse.com
Phone: 833-262-8899

Published by AuthorHouse 03/17/2022

ISBN: 978-1-6655-5244-8 (sc)
ISBN: 978-1-6655-5242-4 (hc)
ISBN: 978-1-6655-5243-1 (e)

Library of Congress Control Number: 2022903159

Print information available on the last page.

Any people depicted in stock imagery provided by Getty Images are models, and such images are being used for illustrative purposes only. Certain stock imagery © Getty Images.

This book is printed on acid-free paper.

Because of the dynamic nature of the Internet, any web addresses or links contained in this book may have changed since publication and may no longer be valid. The views expressed in this work are solely those of the author and do not necessarily reflect the views of the publisher, and the publisher hereby disclaims any responsibility for them.

To Les Gandy and James Boynton, the two
educators who influenced me most.
For Lucy Aguilar. Without her, there would be no book.

Contents

POEMS

I Think I'll Major in Education

They said, "Choose a major for college.
You have to make a decision."
I said, "It can't be math.
I stopped at long division."

I recall the colony at Jamestown.
I know of the Roanoke mystery,
But that's all I remember.
I guess it won't be history.

My geography is fuzzy.
I think my maps were too old.
I confuse my facts
About the North and South Poles.

For me, attempting English
Would be a bit absurd.
I never did like Shakespeare.
I can't conjugate a verb.

I never complete a science project
To anyone's satisfaction,
But when I kiss my girlfriend,
There's a chemical reaction.

A firm grasp of any subject
Seems just beyond my reach.
I think I'll major in education.
I feel qualified to teach.

POEMS ABOUT BASKETBALL AND OTHER SPORTS

A Basketball Challenge

She said, "Your chance are slim and none.
Your team cannot beat mine."
I said, "Tell old Slim to suit on up.
I'll take him anytime."

Grateful for Graduation

Neches won State for three straight years.
They haven't been heard from since.
Graduation is a great equalizer.
For it, there is no defense.

An Exciting Ending

The game was decided at the buzzer.
The ball swished right through the net.
Some people were glad.
Some people were sad.
It depended on which way they'd bet.

Play the Next Play

———

Don't fret if you miss a layup.
There's nothing you need to say.
Basketball is a game of mistakes.
Move on═play the next play.

Don't react to the referees.
You won't change their minds anyway.
Not many games are lost from one call.
Move on═play the next play.

Always shoot when you're open.
If the ball doesn't fall, it's okay.
Have a short memory and shoot it again.
Move on═play the next play.

It doesn't matter if you're in peewee,
Play in college, or the NBA.
At every level, the game is the same.
Move on═play the next game.

A Gifted Scorer

———

A shooter like Steph Curry
There has never been before.
Some of his threes are so far out
They should actually count for four.

Whatever Happened to the Post Man?

Three-pointers can blow a game open.
The change can be abrupt.
Percentages are better near the basket.
Can anyone post up?
If you look at the history of the NBA,
The lesson is clear as can be.
Kareem is the all-time leading scorer.
I doubt that he ever made a three.

The Problem with Being Short

"It was an accident by inches,"
The athlete told the cop.
"An outfielder's legs
Could have reached those brakes,
But me, I play shortstop."

Clyde Drexler

He played the game eight hours a day.
His obsession was almost pathetic.
It took him to the Hall of Fame.
His success was not genetic.

Call Me the Correct Name

I've beaten you ten times straight.
On you, I've left my stamp.
You call me a bad name after each game.
Why not just call me "Champ"?

For an All-State Player

I know a girl named Maggie Peacock.
She's an athlete; there's no doubt.
Her primary reason for basketball success:
Peacock's seldom *fowl* out.

For Chelsea

Some players can score easily.
Some players simply cannot.
You are a great shooter.
I think you must practice a *Lott*.

For Kaylee and Kaymee Little

Both of you shoot really well.
You both can take a charge.
Your last name may be Little,
You don't just play big;
You play large.

A Reluctant Fan

It broke my heart
When y'all moved to Lipan.
I remember how much it hurt.
I watched you win State on the iPad.
I was wearing a Lipan shirt.

For Taylor Clark

I know it hurt when you got hurt.
It sent your life into a skid.
But there would be no State title without you.
You earned it as much as they did.

For Marty Seymour

There has seldom been a girl this quick.
There has seldom been a girl this fast.
If you go see her play,
Each time you'll *Seymour.*
If you race her,
You'll probably see last.

For Taylor Branson

It's hard to be a basketball player
When you have a talented brother.
It's hard to be a basketball player
When your coach is also your mother.
It's hard when you have to shoot in the cold.
It's hard when you shoot in the sun.
But I seriously doubt that you'll find it hard
To wear the State ring that you won.

An Absentee Fan

Because of the virus, I didn't see the team play.
Nobody ever said life was fair.
I don't claim to be the best fan in Lipan,
But I'm the best one who wasn't there.

Mama Was Wrong

When I was due to get my college diploma,
There was an awkward situation.
I was watching the ABA Finals,
So I skipped my graduation.

My mother said, "You're not going?
I think that is a shame."
I said, "Mama, I have to stay here.
They're playing the seventh game."

She glared at me and said, "Robert,
I think this choice you'll later regret."
It's been fifty years- I still remember that game.
I haven't been sorry yet.

A Job Offer

She said, "They came and asked me to coach.
I said, "I don't think you're ready."
She said, "I don't think so either,
But the paycheck will be steady."

She's gone to State seven of eleven times.
The school is satisfied for now.
I just wonder how well she will do
After she's had time to learn how.

Practice Makes Perfect

He said, "You always beat me.
Could you tell me why that's true?"
I said, "There's a simple answer.
I practice more than you."

You say you detest your rivals.
It makes you sick when you lose to them.
There's a remedy for your illness:
Get a ball and find a gym.

Remember that the one who wins
Is the one who can brag and boast.
Remember that the one who wins
Is the one who works the most.

For Trinity

They say you would start for many schools,
And I'm sure that you could.
You added a dimension to this team
That really made them good.
Most of your teammates are older.
They will get and deserve attention.
But they can't bring up the State title
Unless your name is mentioned.

The Reason I Can Shoot

He said, "You shoot the ball so well.
Is there a secret to it?"
I said, "I practice all the time.
That's the reason I can do it.
If you aim that ball just above the net,
It'll usually go right through it."

A Talented Player

_____

He discovered basketball
At the beginning of third grade.
He found a hoop and some friends,
And every day they played.

Most went home right after school,
But he always stayed.
His dad promised him a dollar
For every hundred shots he made.

Sometimes he had to get an extra job
To make sure the boy was paid.
On his seventeenth birthday,
The State championship was played.

His opponents could not stop him.
They were all dismayed.
He won an MVP and the title.
His full talent was displayed.

Football Dreams

She said, "I'll sleep with the entire team.
I'll bet you that I can."
He said, "It shouldn't be too hard.
We only play Six-Man."

Randy Spain 1974

Sometimes when we get nostalgic,
We talk about our exes.
He was the best player on the team
The day we won the State of Texas.

Randy Spain was so good for so long that the fans even took him for
granted. However, if his opponents did this, they always paid dearly.
Huckabay never had a player like Randy Spain.

Andy Wartes 1965

His hair was blonde,
But his skin was dark.
He was a handsome kid.
I never saw anyone shoot a ball
Exactly like he did.

Any time we played Lipan,
It always caused a buzz.
I couldn't name their players,
But I knew who Wartes was.

Lipan had good players.
He could have been called great.
Had the school been better known,
He would have been All-State.

We put our best player on him.
He handled it just fine.
It was like a grown man playing with boys.
It almost blew my mind.

His combination of school and talent
Made him extremely rare.
If you looked at Major college
You'd find his equal there.

Playing good opponents doesn't always work out,
But sometimes it does.
Anyone who saw him play,
Knew who Wartes was.

POEMS ABOUT FAMILY

The Advantage of Heredity

The ability of his descendants
Cannot be overstated.
If Jimmy Tate were a race horse,
He would be syndicated.

Family Resemblance

His dad was a good-looking giant.
His mom was a wicked witch.
He resembled both of his parents.
He was a big, handsome, son-of-a _____.

A Mother's Discipline

My mother whipped me quite often.
I did not like the pain.
I said, "Don't hit me too hard.
I have a damaged brain."

I expected she would laugh.
Instead she gave me a smirk.
She said, "Robert, your brain is just fine.
It's your attitude that needs work."

An Unusual Family

She had a thing for men,
But she was kind of mannish.
Her brothers were all handsome,
But they were kind of clannish.

They all spoke three languages:
English, French, and Spanish.
When a cop came close to any of them,
They could quickly vanish.

For a Close Relative

My age and health
Brought a burden to my family.
My body has betrayed me, not my mind.
My cousin says I'm a nuisance to everyone.
He says I bother folks all the time.
I really can't do much to change this.
I admit what he says is true.
I have only one answer to his statement:
Someday, he'll get old too.

Something Better

Had I known I'd be childless when I was young,
It would have broken my heart to pieces.
But now I have something better than kids of my own.
I have my nephews and my nieces.

Sometimes You Can
Know Too Much

I said, "I want to learn about my family.
I want to know where I came from."
I spent some time and some money
On a site called Ancestry.com.

I found that my folks were farmers.
I saw that some of them taught school.
I also learned several other things
That really weren't too cool.

I now believe the past
Might be better left alone.
Some things we think we need to know
Are better left unknown.

A Dedicated Parent

His daughter was extremely fast.
She ran three events in track.
His son was both big and strong.
He was the quarterback.
He made them practice every day.
He never cut them slack.
It wasn't fun to play, so they ran away.
Neither one of them came back.

In Search of a Parent

His mom met a man on the internet
And left for Texas City.
His dad lived in Austin and drank a lot.
His future wasn't pretty.

They put him in an orphan's home.
They said it would be stable.
He was taught to iron his clothes
And have manners at the table.

He graduated high school early.
He was only seventeen.
He was about the smartest kid
That home had ever seen.

He didn't leave for college.
He left to locate his mother.
He found her with two more children.
He had a sister and a brother.

He hoped to help her raise them.
But the environment there was bad.
He finally left for Austin.
He was searching for his dad.

My Cousin Ricky

Cousin Lou Ann was like my sister.
She lived with us as a child.
She's married with three children.
Her son is kind of wild.

From the second he was born,
He was smart and sort of tricky.
She could have named him after me;
Instead she called him Ricky.

I've treated him as a nephew.
We're still close today.
He takes advantage of me.
I like him anyway.

He's done a lot of good things
And some that weren't quite right.
He's not our family's black sheep,
But he's sure not Snow White.

Despite his imperfections,
I still hold him dear.
He's part of our family.
I'm lucky that he's here.

When God Made Brady Nelson

When God made Brady Nelson
He made the cutest boy.
We loved him from the first;
He was our pride and joy.

When God made Brady Nelson
He put a big smile on our face.
Every child after him
Came in second place.

Reluctant Acceptance

We inherit our physical appearance.
There's not much we can do to change it.
But often when I look in the mirror,
I'd like to rearrange it.

Unique First Names

Today, folks need a thesaurus
To choose a name for their baby.
My friend called her triplet daughters
Almost, Perhaps, and Maybe.

An Incident with a Gun

He said, "Dad, I don't want to hunt."
But his father didn't hear.
He said, "Shoot that buck when it gets close.
Hand me another beer.
If I didn't know you better, boy,
I'd think that you were queer."
So he shot his dad with the rifle
That was meant for shooting deer.
Then he turned himself into the cops
And never shed a tear.

A Common Occurrence

The girl showed us to the office.
She looked at me sort of funny.
She said to my sister,
"What's the matter with him, honey?"
Sis replied, "He has a birth defect.
It's hard for him to walk.
But address your questions straight to him.
I promise he can talk."

Aaron and Some of the People Who Love Him (December 1999)

———————

Aaron Robert Callaway is this young man's name.
He's been a joy to our family since the moment he came.
How well I remember the birth of this guy.
He came one day after the Fourth of July.
I know when they called us, the phone rang just twice.
Grandma Sarah said, "A boy…how neat. Well, how nice!"
So we each went to see him as quick as we could.
And we all prophesied that at sports he'd be good.
And he sure seems to be, though he's really quite young.
We're still eagerly waiting for what he'll become.

Aaron's good at all games. He's ahead of the rest.
The sport that's in season is the one he likes best.
He plays soccer and baseball and rides in rodeos.
He's won lots of trophies; he'll tell you about those.
He'll be good at round ball; he just might be great.
He'll sure have to play it; his mom was a Tate.
But his future's in football. I'll say that myself.
Someday he'll make touchdowns like his Uncle Jeff.
He jumps so high, and he runs so well.
Someday he might play in the NFL.

Aaron has two cousins named Brady and Zach.
When these three get together, it's wild how they act.
They're all so excited, you can't calm them down.
It's as if they're all walking four feet from the ground.
Sometimes they're Indians; sometimes they're cowboys.
But whatever they play, they make lots of noise.
They never get bored. They'd play on forever.
They never grow tired of being together!
And I like to watch them, though they're often too loud.

I always remember, *Grandma Sarah would be proud!*
When Aaron's mother's at work, he stays with his granny.
He has a name for her; he calls her "My Danny."
She helped to make certain that he got a good start.
I think she's one reason that he is so smart.
Rhonda is another grandmother he's got.
He calls her "My Nana" and likes her a lot.
On the guy side, there's Gramps, and Pa, and Jimmy too.
When it comes to grandfathers, he's got quite a few.
It's probably obvious, but I'll just mention
That Aaron Robert never lacks love or attention.

Aaron likes to go to Aunt Linda's farm.
He jumps at the house. He runs at the barn.
He gets his Aunt Tommie to help him build pens.
They corral his animals again and again.
Sometimes they roast wieners; sometimes they fly kites.
They read lots of books, 'cause that's what he likes.
Aaron always has energy and he loves to play.
He'd never go home; he'd just stay and stay.
The farm is not fancy but the admission is free.
And Aaron sure thinks it's a fine place to be.

POLITICAL POEMS

A One-Word President

If Trump has a vocabulary,
He keeps it all to himself.
His favorite word must be *very*.
Quite often he says nothing else.

An Opinion of the President

Trump has no integrity.
I think he lies all the time.
If he gave me his word and two nickels,
All I would have is a dime.

Why He Shouldn't Run Again

Trump will be so old by 2024,
To run again would be dumb.
If he gets to go back to the White House,
He'll leave the nursing home to come.

A Hypocritical Response

Trump said the virus wasn't serious.
He made fun of masks a lot.
But when he got sick,
He got the best medicine,
And now he has taken the shot.

An Assault on Our Capitol

The rioters stormed the Capitol.
They wanted to kill Mike Pence.
It's a shame when the center of a democracy
Is surrounded by a fence.
The rioters stormed the Capitol,
And Trump put them up to it.
Then he came out on TV
And swore he didn't do it.

A Grandpa Who Changed

Frank was a staunch Republican.
He stood for law and order.
He wanted to keep all Mexicans
On their side of the border.

He didn't believe in ESL.
He found it unnecessary.
There was not a Spanish word
In his vocabulary.

His son began dating a dark-haired girl.
She was a resident.
I think it happened the first year
That Trump was president.

Three months into their relationship,
She was found to be with child.
When Frank found out about it,
He went about half wild.

The baby is walking and talking now.
He's cute and that's a fact.
He simply adores his grandpa,
And Grandpa loves him back.

Frank changed his thoughts on immigration.
He feels people don't need to "stay home."
He said, "You view Mexicans differently
When you get one of your own."

POEMS ABOUT ANIMALS

Nobody Gets Along
on the Tate Farm

The gobbler doesn't like the rooster.
The rooster doesn't like the buck.
Nobody gets along on the Tate Farm.
The hen doesn't like the duck.

The donkey doesn't like the pony.
The pony doesn't like the cow.
Nobody gets along on the Tate Farm.
The boar doesn't like the sow.

The peacock doesn't like the puppy.
The puppy doesn't like the cat.
Nobody gets along on the Tate Farm.
The mouse doesn't like the rat.

The goat doesn't like the mosquito.
The mosquito doesn't like the flea.
Nobody gets along on the Tate Farm.
I'm surprised my wife likes me.

This acrimony among my animals
Has really got me stumped.
They fight like rival politicians.
I can't blame this on Trump.

No Need to Be Hasty

My new dog ate my book
About Harry Potter.
I was so upset
I took my gun and shot her.
Now I have no book.
I have no dog.
I wish I'd never got her.

Color Preference

I love Appaloosas.
I like paint horses too.
But if you don't like palominos,
There's something wrong with you.

Less Chance for Error

I call my new dog by my own name.
The reason for this is,
If I can remember the name Mom called me,
I can probably remember his.

The Chicken-Egg Argument

Which came first,
The hen or the egg?
Did it rain before it snowed?
If you don't want to see
Feathers flying through the air,
Keep your chickens out of the road.

An Unusual New Neighbor

Linda and Leroy were leery
When their new neighbor came along.
He had a peacock that screamed,
A donkey that brayed,
And a parrot that sang dirty songs.

An Envious Lamb

———

The lamb looked longingly across the fence.
All she could do was stare.
She said, "The grass is greener on that side.
I wish that I lived there.

I need to find a way to get through.
I mean golly, gosh, gee whiz."
Her mom said, "You may think it's better over there,
But that doesn't mean it is.

You think that place would be Heaven,
But that's all in your head.
The way you covet that green grass
Is enough to make me see red.

Little Bo Peep lost her sheep,
And that pasture was where they went.
She left them alone, but they never came home.
You should stay here and be content."

She said, "*Ewe* should learn a lesson, little girl lamb.
Ewe would do well to listen to me.
Green grass is good, but you're green with envy.
That's never a good way to be."

What the Hen Said

The hen was angry with the rooster.
She chased him from the pen.
She said, "You crowed so loud this morning.
You woke me up again."
He said, "Crowing is my main job.
That's all that there is to it."
She said, "My main job is laying eggs.
Without sleep, I can't do it."

What the Cat Said

The cat threw the mouse in the air.
She was really having fun.
She grabbed him when he hit the ground
And repeated what she'd done.

He said, "If you keep doing this,
You'll have to call a nurse.
I've had a migraine for three days.
You're making it much worse."

The cat didn't slow down a bit.
She just gave a little purr.
She said, "I can eat you for lunch,
Or throw you in the air.
Which do you prefer?"

A Dog's Life

————

The cow stared at the dog.
The dog stared at the cow.
He said, "It's easier on both of us
If you start home right now."

She said, "You are right, wise dog.
And I'm about to go.
But there's a lot of grazing over here.
Can we please take it slow?"

He replied, "Of course we can.
There's no need to be quick.
When I'm through with you, all I have to do
Is fetch somebody's stick."

She said, "Doesn't that bother you?
If it does not, it should."
He said, "It's either that or chase a cat.
A dog's life ain't too good.

"Sometimes people have me do tricks
Simply because they're spiteful."
She said, "Yes they do, and compared to you,
My life is *udder*ly delightful."

Ode to a Dead Red Rabbit (1974)

Sandy Brown,
Buck of renown,
Leaped from his pen
And fell to the ground.
A dog crept up
Without a sound.
And that was the end of Sandy Brown.
Fur and bones were all we found.

Bo Peep and the Inebriated Sheep

Little Bo Peep
Had lost her sheep.
You've heard all this before.
She found them down
In a bad part of town.
They were at the liquor store.
The bartender smiled
When she arrived.
He said, "Hello, Miss Bo Peep.
I'm glad it's you.
What shall we do
With all these drunken sheep?"

People Act Like Sheep or Vice Versa

Mary had a little lamb.
You've probably heard the story.
She washed and combed its fleece each day.
The wool was its shining glory.

Some in the flock were jealous
Because it got so much attention.
They called that lamb a lot of names
It would be unkind to mention.

Trump showed us when people act like sheep,
The results can be a disaster.
But when sheep act like people,
Things can turn bad even faster.

Zachary and the Goats
(November 1999)

There's a little boy; his name is Zach.
His hair is red, his eyes are black.
He loves the game of basketball.
But he likes Linda's farm the best of all.

There are lots of goats that must be fed.
He owns Black Coffee and brother Red.
Some drink a bottle and gulp it down.
Others nurse their mothers and dance around.

There's Streak who's bad and Stripe who's nice.
There's even one called Vanilla Ice.
There's Apache who gets too rough when he plays.
There's a white one named Blondie and a new one called Blaze.

There's Coffee who comes when you call her name.
And Licorice Lady and Lacy Jane.
There's Dancer, the mother of most of the rest.
And Champion, who's mean and milks with the best.

There's Corky, who likes to jump and to skip.
There's Tar Baby with her odd, funny lip.
There's Pretty Girl and Rachel with their dappled hides.
There's Golden Surprise, who is Linda's pride.

The goats need care through summer and snow.
When Zach gets to Linda's, he's ready to go.
He feeds them and leads them and rides them too.
There's not too much she won't let him do.

Zach helps Linda doctor; he helps trim their feet.
He brushes their coats till they're shiny and neat.
He smiles when they run and laughs when they play.
Zach never gets tired; he'd watch goats all day.

When Zach grows up, he's made up his mind.
He's building a dairy and milking full-time.
He'll pen up his goats and run them right through.
That's pretty big plans for a little boy of two.

His grandpa will help him, and maybe his mother.
He says he'll hire Linda and his baby brother.
You can't ever tell; he might do it too.
Wouldn't it just be dandy if his dreams came true?

Brady and Some of His Friends (December 1999)

There's a little blond boy whose name is Brady.
He has two dogs called Cinnamon and Shady.
They stay at Linda's and she feeds them,
But they both know they belong to him.
Cinnamon's nearly all red. Shady's nearly all gray.
They love for Brady to come over and play.
They bark when they see him. They jump and they run.
He squeals with delight. They all have such fun!
There's none happier than are these three.
This boy and his dogs are something to see!

Brady has two goats. You've heard of them maybe.
The mother's Gray Coffee, and there's Shadow, her baby.
Gray Coffee's a milker; she fills up the pail.
Shadow follows along just wagging her tail.
Brady can't really milk them. He's too little yet.
But someday he'll do it; on that you can bet.
He feeds them with corn. He brings in a can.
Sometimes they eat it right out of his hand.
He sure loves to ride them. It fills him with glee.
This tot and his goats are something to see!

When Brady's at Linda's, he knows no fear.
He pretends he's an Indian hunting coyotes and deer.
He really loves Linda, but Tommie's his pard'.
Sometimes they get brave and sleep in the yard.
They stare at the moon as it beams from on high.
He calls Grandma Sarah the brightest star in the sky.
He lies there intently and listens for danger.
Sometimes he is Tonto waiting for the Lone Ranger.

And when he does go to sleep, he's content as can be.
This lad as an Indian is something to see!

His palomino's named Sugar. She's a beautiful yellow.
When Brady's astride her, he's quite the big fellow.
He's up there just grinning, sitting tall in the saddle.
He pretends he's a ranch hand out checking his cattle.
He hoops and he hollers just to get her to go.
She sighs when he kicks her but still goes really slow.
It's as if she knows precisely the pace that he needs.
When Brady is riding, a trot is top speed.
But she's a race horse to Brady; he's in ecstasy.
This kid as a cowboy is something to see!

Brady has an aunt, and Amber's her name.
He goes to all of her basketball games.
There aren't too many that he hasn't seen.
He's watched her from Lubbock to Abilene.
He gets all excited, and I should report.
He screams out her name as she runs down the court.
The fans in the stands all hear and start grinning.
She waves when she sees him and tries to keep winning.
The coaches even laugh when he gets in a spree.
This tyke at a ball game is something to see!

So now you've met Brady and some of his friends.
Soon you'll have to come and see them again.
Amber will look for you. The dogs and the goats will too.
The horse, deer, and coyotes are waiting for you.
And Brady will greet you with his lovely smile.
I don't think I've seen a friendlier child.
Yes, now you've met Brady, so cute and so clever.
It seems like he has been with us forever.
He's right at the center of what we do now.
We got along before he got here. I just don't know how!

POEMS OF SOCIAL IMPACT

A Plea for Gun Control

He killed himself with a pistol.
He was home when the deed was done.
His note said, "I couldn't have done this
If I had not had a gun."

The incident shocked the community.
He was known to be smart and kind.
But depression isn't visible.
They could not read his mind.

There was a huge crowd at his funeral.
You could see the teardrops glisten.
His death was a plea for gun control,
But no one cared to listen.

It Might Be a Little Too Warm

I don't want to be cremated.
Of that process I want no part.
It'll be hot enough where I'm going.
The devil doesn't need a head start.

A Good Way to Live

He always said, "I can."
He never said, "I can't."
He never made excuses.
He lived life without complaint.

A Common Reaction to Seeing Me

I move so slowly,
When folks see me,
They think that I am ill.
It hurts some of them
To watch me walk.
To me, it's no big deal.

Better to Be Satisfied

I used to fantasize
A miracle would occur,
And I'd be like everyone else.
When I see how some
Of my friends turned out,
I'm glad I stayed myself.

All Things Are Not Tied to Politics

It doesn't matter if your politics
Run to the right or the left.
If I have no gun, I can't shoot you,
And I sure can't shoot myself.

A Colorful Poem

Roses are red.
Violets are blue.
I could also say grass is purple,
But it would not be true.

What Will Be the Next Excuse?

Some people decline the corona vaccine.
They say it might cause trouble that's greater.
So go ahead and skip it.
If you die now,
You won't need it later.
Some simply will not take it.
They say it's just not the answer.
I wonder, would they feel the same way
If we had a shot that stopped cancer?

Glad for Others

If a person is jealous,
Their life is full of stress.
Someone doesn't have to fail
For me to have success.

An Example of Our Spoiled Society

We used to butcher a deer each year
To help us make it through the winter.
Now if our meat isn't from Walmart,
My wife won't even fix dinner.

An Unimportant Person

I thought my decisions would be significant.
I thought they would be iconic.
The most important choice I make each day:
Should it be Whataburger or Sonic?

An Argument for Lower Speed

I think you should adjust your speed.
Slowing down is the thing to do.
Whenever they coined the term roadkill,
They didn't intend it for you.

Be Careful in the Kitchen

I was at my home in the kitchen
When I fell and broke my hip.
I got well and went to Mom's house.
In her kitchen, I had another slip.
The surgeries were quite painful.
There was a lot of cutting and stitchin'.
Perhaps I should walk with a little more care.
Maybe I should stay out of the kitchen.

Spankings Usually Don't Hurt

My mother spanked me hard and quite often.
My brother whipped me when she quit.
I've always worked,
And I've never gone to jail.
I don't think it hurts to be hit.

Different Types of Talents

My sister-in-law is an artist.
I think few things could be cooler.
I could not even draw a square box
Unless I was using a ruler.

Damaged from Childhood

She said, "Do you recognize me?"
I said, "Of course I do."
She said, "When we were children,
I often made fun of you."
I said, "I recall it clearly.
You were the meanest girl I ever knew."

I said, "You warped me badly.
It cannot be denied.
I was released from prison last year.
I'm uncomfortable on the outside.
I see my PO and my shrink each week.
I hope you're satisfied."

She said, "I'm truly sorry
For all the harm I did.
I know that my cruel words
Sent your life into a skid.
I'm a school counselor now.
I'd do anything to help a kid."

I said, "Because of you,
My whole life has been cursed.
When they seek the source of my problem,
Your name comes up first.
I hope you help those school kids.
My condition can't be reversed."

A Lack of Appreciation for Plants

Some people like a well-kept yard.
That's not my cup of tea.
Some like to show off flowers.
That doesn't do much for me.

I appreciate a nice green lawn.
I see why some folks flaunt it.
But if you can't graze it or smoke it,
I really just don't want it.

Try Alcohol Next Time

I was on the stage drinking beer
When something made me fall.
I was so inebriated,
It didn't hurt at all.
The next time you need a pain killer,
I recommend alcohol.

Another Plea for Gun Control

No matter what our political views,
It's pretty plain to see:
If there are no guns,
I can't shoot you,
And you can't shoot me.

A Gun Is Usually Worse

They say guns don't kill people.
They say that people do.
But I can hurt you less with a rock,
Than I can with a .22.

You Can Stay High for Only So Long

Jack was nimble and he was quick.
He could jump high with the best.
But in the end,
Gravity would win.
He lay on the ground
With the rest.

What Would the Victims Say?

———————

They argue if we let the government have our guns,
They're taking our rights away.
But mass-shooting victims had rights too.
They're not here to have a say.

Peace for Our Country

———————

The COVID has slowed down a bit.
Mass shootings have increased.
The cops blame the people.
The people hate police.
If we eliminated guns,
The slaughter just might cease.
I think it is the only way
To bring our nation peace.

An Attempt at Free Enterprise

I needed to make some money,
So I decided to be pragmatic.
I thought I'd supplement my salary;
I'd grow dope inside my attic.
The plants flourished immediately.
I was shocked they did so well.
But I sampled so much of what I grew.
There wasn't much to sell.
My effort at free enterprise
Didn't get me anywhere.
My income is still low.
But I'm so high,
I really just don't care.

An Ode to Politeness

Mrs. Jones had a daughter, Jill.
She had a son named Jack.
They didn't dress or read too well.
But she taught them how to act.
She said, "My kids ain't pretty.
I think they're not too bright.
They may not be most popular,
But at least they are polite."

A Poem about Myself

The child had trouble walking.
He looked a little funny.
If the kids were nice to him,
He gave them all his money.

Being taken advantage of
Would always be his fate.
I'm not sure I recall his name.
I think it was Bobby Tate.

My Mother Was Right

I was a fifteen-year-old boy
Trying to find my way.
Sometimes I drank beer with my friends.
It was our form of play.
My mother said, "Why do you want to drink?
You can't walk anyway."
I didn't understand what she meant then.
But I sure do today.

What a Height Change
Would Have Done

Had I grown six inches taller,
I would have been much stronger.
Had this actually happened,
My crutches would be longer.

My Hero

Tom T. Hall was my idol.
Tom T. Hall still is.
I just wish the verses I write
Were half as good as his.

Too Young to Raise a Child

He parked out on a dirt road.
They began kissing in the car.
Things got a little heated.
They went a little far.

Her education about birth control
Had been somewhat neglected.
The child that resulted
Was certainly unexpected.

She didn't keep the little boy.
She gave him to someone else.
How can you expect to raise a child
If you're a child yourself?

Who Is the Crazy One?

"Mass shooters are insane,"
I heard one broadcaster say.
But are they any crazier
Than the members of NRA?

POEMS ABOUT RELIGION

One More Chance from God

The Lord said to Jesus,
"The world is out of whack."
Jesus said, "I know, Dad.
Why don't You take it back?"
God said, "Folks deserve for the world to end.
It cannot be denied.
But when you're choosing
Who's going to Heaven or Hell,
It's difficult to decide."
He said, "Religion is about redemption.
That's what Your whole life was about.
I think I'll go ahead and give people another chance.
This time they might straighten out."

A Typical Preacher

The hungry man robbed a bank.
The preacher called him a sinner.
Then he took money from the collection plate,
Went out, and bought steak for dinner.

A Bad Deed with a Good Outcome

David was so enamored of Bathsheba.
He caused her husband's death no doubt.
His actions were not wise,
But Solomon certainly was.
Things have a way of working out.

Just Another Church Romance

The preacher could not
Concentrate on his sermon.
He liked the redhead in the front row.
He said, "Let's go to a motel.
My wife will never know."
She smiled at him and winked.
She spoke these words real slow:
"The deacons sent me here
To check up on you.
Let me report to them first.
Then we'll go."

A Question for the Preacher

I donated to the preacher.
He came to visit me.
He said, "Thanks for the money.
You're as generous as can be."

I said, "You're truly welcome.
I'm glad you know where I live.
Where were you those other months
When I had no check to give?"

POEMS ABOUT POEMS

Poems and Plants Keep You Poor

I grow apples in my attic.
I grow broccoli in my basement.
My sheep ate my neighbor's flowers.
I grew their replacement.
I can grow anything with my green thumb.
I can write rhymes night and day.
I know everything about plants and poems,
Except how to make them pay.

A Happy Poet

His poems were so humorous
He was to the king invited.
He only wrote rhymes for money.
He wasn't too excited.
His Majesty gave him a huge tip.
Then he was delighted.
He composed a verse to thank him,
And the kind king had him knighted.

A Poet with a Weak Jaw

Muhammad Ali wrote a lot of poems.
It helped his career a bunch.
I think I write as well as he did,
But I sure can't take a punch.

A Colloquial Poem (1980)

I no longer know
Where good language is "at."
I think it was lost "on accident" "and that."
But perhaps if we study,
And watch how we act,
Good language "and everything"
Will get it "brung" back.

Nostalgia

The yearbook made me nostalgic.
I thought about the past.
I was moved to write a poem for you.
How did time go by so fast?
Then I recalled you'd left me,
And my poetic inclination diminished.
Since you won't be here to read it,
I have no reason to _____.

POEMS ABOUT LOVE

Which Choice?

She met him.
She loved him.
She left him.
He could not convince her to stay.
She would be better off
Had she kept him.
But she could not function that way.
We always talk about good choices.
Seldom do we mention the bad.
Inside her head, she heard voices.
A bad choice wasn't the best choice,
But it was the best choice she had.

A Case of Mistaken Identity

It wasn't how she left him
That caused his heart to break.
She cheated while they were together.
That was really hard to take.
It's not what a person says.
It's what a person does.
That woman wasn't exactly
The person he thought she was.

A Disappointing Romance

___

He met her in spring training,
The year he was a rookie.
She had long black hair
And dark brown eyes.
Her brother was a bookie.
He said, "The odds are five to one
She'll get him to the altar."
She led him to the church
Like she had a rope and halter.
She said, "Once you have me,
You'll never want another."
Then she spent his signing bonus
And went home to her mother.

An Unclothed Investigation

___

He tracked them to a hotel room.
His detective work was a success.
He found them there without their clothes.
Their intent wasn't hard to guess.
He said, "It's none of my business,
But if I may suggest,
Since I'm about to notify your spouses,
You probably should get dressed."

No Better the Second Time

I said, "Your new husband's no winner.
I can see that for myself."
She said, "I agree he's a loser,
But so was the one I just left."

A Slow Learner

I never do well with women.
Women never do well with me.
After seventy years, I figured it out.
Marriage just isn't for me.

Practical Chemistry

She didn't understand science.
She didn't grasp neutron diffraction.
But in the back seat of her boyfriend's car,
She caused a chemical reaction.

She Fooled the Judge

_____

We dated nearly two years.
She said, "Let's rob that station.
We'll make our getaway.
That money can be spent in Mexico.
There'll be enough to play.
I've been meaning to learn Spanish.
It's the best language anyway."

I tried to be casual as we did it.
The cashier saw right through it.
She quickly called the police.
We were caught before we knew it.
The tape showed her holding a gun.
The jury did not review it.
She told the judge with soft doe eyes,
"My boyfriend made me do it."

Saturday Night Date

_____

He said, "Let's go a little further.
We'll have a little bit more fun."
The fun they had is in first grade now.
They're both really proud of their son.

A Surprise for Mary

Mary married Mike for his money.
Or at least she thought she did.
She never told anyone about it.
She thought she kept it hid.

She put up with infidelity.
She endured verbal abuse.
She never once thought of leaving.
His money was her excuse.

When he died and the will was probated,
Mary was in for a shock.
Mike didn't have any money,
And he'd liquidated all his stocks.

"He told me he hated you," said her mother-in-law.
"And I guess he meant it.
He knew you married him for his money.
He gave me all he had and I spent it."

Plain Jane (Written 2011)

She met him at the senior prom
On a night when she felt quite sad.
Being a Plain Jane, she hadn't wanted to come.
But when she saw him, she was happy she had.

Looking handsome and hip, he asked her to dance,
And her heart quivered like jelly.
He said, "Tonight, I'll expand your mind."
Instead he expanded her belly.

And now she lies in a hospital bed,
Anxiously awaiting delivery.
She thinks of him, but this time
It's her stomach, not her heart, that feels quivery.

As for him, he's left her alone
To bear the fruit of their brief romance.
Right now, he's at a party on the other side of town,
And he's asking this Plain Jane to dance.

Try to Pick a Rich Girl

My mother told me,
"Boy, I wish you'd settle down.
You seem to have more girlfriends
Than anyone around."
I said, "You are right.
It cannot be denied.
I know I need only one,
But I just can't decide."
She said, "I can't choose for you,
But I'll tell you something, sonny.
Poor girls often make poor wives,
So try to pick one with money."

Good Luck to Both of You

You cheated on me with a friend of mine.
It was right before my eyes.
I hope it works out for you both.
If not, don't be surprised.

A Full Circle

In this strange life,
Many things often run full course.
I bought a cool shirt for my wedding.
I also wore it to my divorce.

Happy Birthday to Pam

I acknowledge a lot of birthdays.
I think you know that's true.
But when it came to yours this year,
I didn't know what to do.

I thought of reaching you by phone,
But something made me balk.
On the rare times that I call you,
You never have time to talk.

I could not find you a funny card
With a fancy verse and glitter.
You know I don't do Facebook,
And I sure can't do Twitter.

You say you're too fat for candy.
You would ridicule a flower.
And you wouldn't go out to eat with me,
Unless I paid you by the hour.

Once, we would have gone for a drive.
But you won't get that invitation.
If someone saw us together,
It might hurt your reputation.

We couldn't go to Senior Citizens.
Of that there is no chance.
Since you want me in a wheelchair,
I don't think we could dance.

I could buy you a bright new dress.
But I doubt that you would wear it.
And you wouldn't accept a diamond,
No matter what the carat.

If I offer to give you cash,
You make me feel inept.
I'll have to keep my money
So you won't feel you're kept.

You've created a dilemma, Pam.
The options left are few.
You won't like this poem either,
But happy sixty-ninth to you.

Edna-Forever

_____

She told me she would love me forever,
So I asked her to be mine.
She said that we would always be together,
But forever was just a short time.

Forever didn't last very long for Edna.
I never knew that forever would end.
I wonder why she told me those lies.
But I bet she'd retell them if I asked her again.

Ode to an Ex-Wife

_____

Edna Sheryl, you're quite a witch.
You get a man and then you switch.
You pull this off without a hitch.
I hope somebody don't snitch.

A Fortunate Bonus

She asked me to be her boyfriend.
I wasn't too excited.
I told my mom about it.
She seemed to be delighted.

She said, "You mind your P's and Q's,
And make a good impression.
Her dad owns half of Texas;
Buying land is his obsession."

I did as Mama told me.
I didn't want to fail.
He wanted to buy a son-in-law.
I guess I was for sale.

Twenty years and four kids later,
Things haven't turned out bad.
I was a great sperm donor.
I am an okay dad.

Each day, I read all I can
From the world of real estate.
My office is the golf course.
I usually show up late.

My mom is still elated.
She's been known to declare,
"You could have wed a waitress
Or a girl who fixes hair."

Instead, she has rich grandkids.
She couldn't love them more.
She tells them, "Thank your father.
You could have been born poor."

A Nursing Home Poem

The therapist looked down at me.
She said, "Tell me where to start."
I said, "I can't move either leg,
And I have a broken heart."

She gently touched me on the leg.
She said, "I'll fix this for you.
If you give your heart to Jesus,
He'll fix that part too."

I lay there thinking of you
And all the times we shared.
I thought that I was dying.
I've never been that scared.

In the moment I was weakest,
I pretended you were near.
Your hand softly brushed my cheek.
You told me not to fear.

I thought of my life without you,
And I prayed to die.
But the Lord would not take me.
I really don't know why.

For you, I was never good enough.
I wish that wasn't true.
When I believed I was facing death,
My thoughts were still of you.

Natural Chemistry

The theory of relativity
Was invented by Einstein,
But the chemistry between the sexes
Has been here for some time.

An Easy Last Name

She called and said she loved me.
I told her that was good.
She said, "Let's go get married."
I said, "I guess we could."

We saw the preacher the next day.
He encouraged us to wait.
He said, "Why would you want to marry
Someone like Bobby Tate?"

She had an answer ready.
She gave a quick retort.
She said, "Just try and spell Zollenhoffeur.
I want a name that's short."

The Boxer's Wife

She came to me one Friday night.
She said, "Let's fool around."
I said, "You have a husband."
She said, "He's out of town."

Her husband was a boxer.
His talent was reknown.
I pictured myself with two black eyes.
I prudently turned her down.

POETIC TRIBUTES

For Larry Hailey (On Your 75th Birthday)

If a judge gave you seventy-five years in prison,
You'd think the sentence was a stiff one.
If you had a brick made of gold that weighed seventy-five pounds,
I doubt that you could lift one.

If you lost seventy-five pounds on a diet that you tried,
You would be a whole lot thinner.
If you needed a dollar to get a grand prize,
Three quarters wouldn't make you a winner.

There are many things you can do with the number seventy-five.
Some of them are silly or sappy.
You just received a poem from the great Bobby Tate.
I hope that your birthday was happy.

Happy Birthday to Bill Davis (2021)

I write to tell of someone
Who is honest, smart, and kind.
His name is Bill Davis.
He is a friend of mine.

If I did not speak about him,
I would be remiss.
They don't make men like him these days;
They simply don't exist.

He could have done most anything.
His IQ is quite high.
A doctor or a lawyer.
A pilot in the sky.

But he chose his occupation
When he was still a kid.
He decided to work on cars,
And work on cars he did.

If your vehicle has a problem,
He can diagnose it right away.
He's the best mechanic in Texas,
Perhaps the USA.

He can take a truck others scrap for junk
And make it run again.
If Bill Davis can't fix it,
You'd best just trade it in.

He is one of the finest people
I have known in my life.
The only other one even close
Is the girl who is his wife.

I don't know where his talent came from.
I think it was Heaven-sent.
If the White House ran off a motor,
Bill Davis would be president.

Happy Birthday to Nikki
(April 29, 2021)

———————

I recall Jimmy's face when you were born.
His happiness shone through.
I don't think a father ever loved a child
As much as he did you.

Your coming was unexpected.
Your arrival caused a bit of a stir.
From the moment Linda saw you,
She thought you belonged to her.

You brought our family pride on the ball court
And in the classroom too.
I bragged about you all the time.
You're the smartest kid I ever knew.

You're a great mother and great sister.
You are also a good wife.
I don't know where I'd be right now
If you weren't in my life.

Your kindness to Tommie and me
Is something I won't forget.
When I'm gone, you can look back
And have not one regret.

I thought I would write this rhyme
Since it's your birthday.
You remind me of your dad and my mother.
That's the nicest thing I can say.

I like a lot of people,
But you're part of a special few.
I don't think I've ever told you,
But Nikki, I love you.

Happy Birthday, Donna

The twenty-fourth came.
The twenty-fourth went.
Your birthday one more time.
Since I didn't give a gift,
I thought I'd send this rhyme.

During all the time I've known you,
You have been quite kind.
Even through my tough times,
You stayed a friend of mine.
I appreciate the food you've brought.
It helped to get me through.
Your family is so lucky
To have someone like you.

I've never seen a grandma
Who does the things you do.
When someone says you're sweet,
Their statement is quite true.

I recall your mother fondly.
I never will forget her.
If she were here with us now,
The virus would upset her.

It's almost time for your next birthday.
I'm so late with this letter.
Maybe the COVID will go away,
And next year will be better.

For Brandi Nelson on Her Birthday

I remember the day when you were born.
It almost made me mad.
I had to milk your daddy's cows
Because he was so glad.

You were the prettiest baby I had seen
Whose last name was Tate.
I told your father, "She looks good."
He answered, "She looks *great*."

You were bright, sweet, and funny.
Linda claimed you from the start.
My mother rocked you all the time.
You completely stole her heart.

You learned everything we gave you,
It didn't matter what.
Your teacher in the first grade
Said, "She sure knows a lot."

You were good at every game,
But you most liked basketball.
You were like a coach on the floor.
You understood it all.

You could have become about anything
That you desired to be:
A teacher, a doctor, a lawyer,
An announcer on TV.

You gave us Zach and Brady,
And then you got us Ben.
There never were three boys like those,
And there won't be again.

And now we have Callan Tate.
When I saw him, I was hooked.
Every time he laughs or smiles,
I remember how you looked.

On your birthday, I hope your cup of joy
Is full to the brim.
A lot of people love you,
And I am one of them.

Lucy's Children

I have a friend named Lucy.
I've known her for a while.
The first time that I met her,
She was just a child.

Now she has kids of her own:
Army, Josie, and Emma.
She often leaves them home alone.
That creates a dilemma.

She is a real good mom.
She doesn't like to do it.
But circumstance requires it.
That's all there is to it.

She treats them with respect.
She treats them with compassion.
She tries to make them mind.
Nowadays, that's out of fashion.

They'll all be successful;
Of that there is no doubt.
I wish I could live long enough
To see how they turn out.

They could be docs or lawyers.
One might teach school.
One might even be president.
That really would be cool.

Whatever they do in life,
They'll take care of each other.
They'll be kind and good people.
They'll be just like their mother.

POEMS ABOUT
EDUCATION

Ode to a Loyal Teacher

When I die, I may not go to Heaven.
I don't know if they'll let teachers in.
If they don't, just let me go to Huckabay.
But let it be a year when the ball team wins.

Advantage of a Small Class

I was valedictorian.
My cousin was next behind me.
Our rank didn't impress our family;
Our whole class contained only three.

An Aid for Correct Addition

I know my numbers pretty well by now.
Seldom do I miss any.
If I count on my fingers and include my toes,
I can get all the way to twenty.

A Reason for Moving to Texas

I said, "I'm moving to Houston."
Granddad said, "Don't be a fool.
In Arkansas, people who are mentally ill
Go to Texas and teach school."

Two Unimportant Toes

I added up the toes on both my feet.
The number eight was the full amount.
I guess I thought my little toes
Were both too small to count.

A Way to Improve Education

The history teacher was handsome.
The young science teacher was cool.
He invited her to have a drink with him
One day after school.

They spoke of how rude their students were.
Just venting brought elation.
After three margaritas,
They trashed their administration.

They confided in each other.
They swore secrets would be kept.
Alcohol won't save education,
But on some days it can help.

A Modern-Day Education

The fourth-grade student asked the teacher,
"Will you help me find this fact?"
She said, "Check my teacher's guide.
The answers are in the back."

She asked, "Can you show me about my English?
I want to do my best."
She said, "You'll have to help yourself.
I'm preparing for the STAAR test."

She couldn't do her science,
So she put it off till later.
And since she couldn't multiply,
She used a calculator.

She was working on history
When there was a computer crash.
She had completed none of her homework,
But it was the end of class.

A Troublesome Name

Mrs. Bottom had a daughter.
Her first name was Shiny.
The kids gave her a nickname.
They called her Shiny Hiney.

She was a discipline problem.
The principal didn't know what to do.
He said, "If I had a name like hers,
I'd stay in trouble too."

An Ironic Picture

I wrote his English papers.
I did his geometry.
If we had a science project,
He always came to me.

He was recruited for football.
He got a scholarship to play.
I quit college to help my mom
When my dad passed away.

He's superintendent in a huge school district.
His future is secure and bright.
I'm a custodian at the school where we grew up.
This picture doesn't seem quite right.

On Being Placed in the Hall of Honor

_____

When they gave me an award for teaching,
They really threw me a curve.
My colleagues didn't congratulate me.
They knew it was undeserved.

I can't help that the committee chose me.
If I was selected, so be it.
But I placed the plaque
In a room at my house
Where no one else could see it.

A High School Romance

Jack was a first-year teacher.
He liked his English student.
He longed to ask her out,
But felt it was not prudent.

Three days after graduation,
He invited her to the show.
She said, "I've waited all year for this.
I'll be glad to go."

He said, "Did you know I liked you?"
She said, "Who are you trying to kid?
Not only did I know it;
Everyone in my class did."

He felt like he was in a courtroom
And that he was the defendant.
She said, "The principal knew it too.
So did the superintendent."

She said, "I know it's hard to believe,
But I promise that it's true.
Waiting was as hard for the rest of our school
As it was for me and you."

Maybe He Should Be a Teacher

He's too weak in math for accounting.
Too honest for politics and preaching.
Not smart enough for medical or law school.
He probably should try teaching.

He lacks discipline needed for the army.
He can't act or sing; he doesn't have the voice.
He is morally opposed to the oil field.
Education may be his best choice.

He can't be a plumber or mechanic.
The mere thought of manual labor makes him sweat.
He couldn't sell ice cream in the desert.
I think teaching is his best bet.

He can probably become a teacher.
There isn't that much to it.
There's an art to leading a mediocre life.
He can teach kids how to do it.

Would You Try to Understand?
(Written 1985)

This year, spring weather came early.
It makes it hard to stay at school.
It's tough to have class in room 303.
It's so cramped in there, you can't stay cool.
And that teacher is always talking
About the things that ancient people did.
Doesn't he understand
What we're going through, man?
I wonder, was he ever a kid?
"Mr. Tate, would you try to understand
Why we don't have time for you?
I've got a date tonight,
And there's a baseball game.
Why am I supposed to care about Charlemagne?
Mr. Tate, would you try to understand?"

I got caught with snuff in the hallway.
Three days sac is what I'm gonna get.
I gotta beat my parents down to the mailbox,
Or they're gonna ground me, I bet.
And the teacher keeps on talking
Like he's the greatest speaker God ever made.
It may work for some,
But I'm not the right one.
My reading level is fifth grade.
"Mr. Tate, would you try to understand
Why we don't have time for you?
My girl's gonna leave me for a guy with a 'Vette.
How am I supposed to care about Marie Antoinette?
Mr. Tate, would you try to understand?"

We got beat out early in football.
Track is all I have left to do.
I run pretty fast,
But if I don't pass this class,
My athletic days are through.
Some teachers just don't get it.
Without sports, school is no fun.
The man walks with a cane,
And it's pretty plain,
I'm sure that he never could run.
"Mr. Tate, would you try to understand
Why we don't have time for you?
If I don't pass your class,
The coach will be mad.
Is it really my fault
That Hitler was bad?
Mr. Tate, would you try to understand?"

Our senior prom will be here really soon.
I think it's week after next.
The teacher doesn't approve of it.
He said the school shouldn't sponsor sex.
But we're not gonna listen to him.
We expect to have a ball.
He's nice to me,
But he's dull as can be.
Was he ever our age at all?
"Mr. Tate, would you try to understand
Why we don't have time for you?
As a man, you're a blast,
But I don't like your class.
I'll be proud when World History is through.
Mr. Tate, would you try to understand?"

Ambition

The teacher said, "You need ambition, boy.
What do you have in mind?"
I said, "I'd like to raise my kids
And read books from time to time."

He said, "That just won't cut it.
That line of thought won't do."
I said, "Well, I guess I could seek success
And go to school like you.

Every day you show us
In your job, you needn't be bright.
How many college hours does it take
To make a kid be quiet?"

A Special Child

_____

They said, "That boy is Special Ed.
That's all that there is to it."
I said, "He sure was special when he fixed my car.
No one else could do it."

They said, "If you observe him closely,
You'll see often he will drool.
Perhaps if we worked with him a bit,
He might get in trade school."

They sent him off to Waco.
The instructors found he could think.
He owns a Ford dealership and a pawnshop.
He drools all the way to the bank.

He owns a new subdivision.
The complex bears his name.
You can't catch him on the weekends.
That's when he flies his planes.

As for those who ridiculed him,
They're still sure they are cool.
They earn a minimum wage to make kids be quiet.
They shouldn't be allowed to teach school.

His Teaching Bonus

He could have been a doctor.
He could have been a lawyer.
He could have traveled land and sea
Like Huck Finn or Tom Sawyer.

But he chose to be a teacher.
He made children hear his voice.
He taught them what they needed.
He didn't give a choice.

He didn't have much money.
He lived in modest houses.
His son wore hand-me-down britches,
His daughters secondhand blouses.

He doesn't know why he taught.
That was just the way it was.
He didn't understand it.
Perhaps the good Lord does.

Some day when the world is ending
And judgment is upon us,
God might show mercy on him.
That will be his teaching bonus.

For an Old Student

———

They asked me to write the parole board
So he could come home early.
I taught him in fourth grade.
Even as a child, he was surly.

I predicted he might go to prison.
He was trouble even then.
It's ironic that they asked me to help get him out.
I was the first to say he'd be in.

SHORT CLIPS

Our neighbors were married in 1936, and they've fought almost every day since. They don't have little spats either. They have battles, and many of them are bitter.

One day, I was asking the wife how she has stood it for so many years. "You might be better off," I advised, "to go ahead and get a divorce."

"Honey, I couldn't do that," she replied. "If I quit now, he'd think he won."

●

I have a blind friend, but he doesn't feel sorry for himself. In fact, he insists that being sightless has certain

advantages. "After all," he says, "did you ever try to count in braille?"

●

The first time I heard Paul Simon sing "Love Me Like a Rock," I asked a friend, "How could you love somebody like a rock?"

"I'm not sure," he replied. "But I bet you'd have to be really *stoned* first."

●

I have a White friend who is quite concerned about the race problem. He doesn't want his children to be prejudiced, so he never makes reference to a person's color in front of them. He considers everybody to be the same.

My friend is pleased with his son's indifference, but he knows it will not last.

Last week, he and his son were in town. As he parked the car, they saw a Black boy running barefoot up the street. The three-year-old pointed at the boy. "He's different from me," he declared.

This is it, my friend thought. *He's finally noticed.* Trying to keep his voice casual, he asked, "What's different about him, son?"

The child looked at the sneakers on his feet and replied, "Well, Daddy, he's not wearing shoes."

●

Some people lose in the game of love. I not only lose, I get shut out.

●

The women where I work are very liberated. So the men never miss a chance to bother them about it.

Last week, one of the girls was going to buy a new car. She had the deal complete, and we were all excited for her. But she arrived the next day and said she had changed her mind. She wasn't buying a car.

"That's just like a woman," one of the men remarked. "They're wishy-washy. They can never make up their mind."

"Do you agree with that?" I asked the woman next to me.

"No, I don't," she declared. "Well, yes I do. Oh, I don't know. He may be partly right."

●

I have a friend with cerebral palsy. He doesn't let it hamper him though. He participates in more activities than most of his friends. People are constantly amazed at him. But he shrugs it off. He says, "Some people are bald, some are fat, and some have cerebral palsy. I just happen to have cerebral palsy." He explains further, "Everyone has a handicap of some kind. It's just that some can overcome it, and some can't. I can."

●

You have to have thick skin to be a writer. You have to take criticism all the time. When you think about it,

it's a lot like being married.

●

My uncle was a stubborn Democrat, and my aunt was a staunch Republican. They canceled each other's vote in every election for twenty years.

Then in the 1960 presidential election, my aunt suddenly switched parties and voted for Kennedy. She told my uncle about it when they arrived home from the polls. "I had to do it," she declared. "I just thought you and I should stop voting against each other."

My uncle's face turned red. "I feel the same way about it you do," he replied. "You see, today I voted for Nixon."

●

When my best friend announced wedding plans, I offered the same advice I give to all prospective bridegrooms: "Don't do it."

He was a little unnerved by my statement and retorted quickly, "But you're a bachelor. How can you be so sure of yourself?"

I didn't answer. I knew I couldn't change his mind.

Four years and three kids later, he came by to see me. Two of his children had the measles, and the other one had been exposed to chickenpox. My friend looked tired and worn. "You know," he said, "for a bachelor, you sure know a lot about marriage."

●

Warren G. Harding, our twenty-ninth president, was an easygoing young man. He was so eager to please that he did almost anything his friends asked. His father rejoiced in his son's good nature, but he felt the boy sometimes went too far. "Warren," he once told him, "you can't say no to anyone. If you were a girl, you'd be in the family way all the time."

●

My friend bought her two-year-old son a doe rabbit for a pet. Since it was his first pet, she had her heart set on letting him name it. "What do you want to name the rabbit, Vic?"

"What you say, Mama?" he replied.

"What do you want to name the rabbit?" she asked again.

The child looked puzzled. "What you say, Mama? I don't understand what you say."

My friend repeated the question several times. The answer was always "What you say?" My friend was not to be denied. She named the rabbit You Say.

•

When my goat gave birth to twin billies, I let my niece have one for a pet. She named it Billy Jack and lavished him with love and attention. With her good care, he grew to be a beautiful animal. But like all goats, he soon became a nuisance.

When my sister-in-law could no longer put up with him, she brought him back to me. I kept Billy Jack for several weeks. He was a real pest, and I decided to eat him.

My brother and his family came for dinner the first time we had goat meat. My mother cautioned us not to mention that we were having goat. She felt my niece and her mother would be squeamish about eating their pet.

The dinner began pleasantly. Our guests had no idea they were eating goat. Then my little brother finished his first helping.

"Can I get you something?" my mother asked.

My brother got a twinkle in his eyes. "Yes," he said. "I need some more meat. Would you pass the Billy Jack?"

•

My brother served in the Army during World War II. He spent much of his hitch in Europe and was involved in several major battles. He was in hand-to-hand combat three times, but he was never injured. However, these experiences made him nervous, and he was glad to get home on furlough.

His first day back, he went to a bar and got into an argument. During the fight that followed, he was stabbed twice and nearly died from loss of blood.

My father visited him in the hospital the next day. "Are you hurt bad, son?" he asked.

My brother smiled weakly. "No, Dad," he said. "I'll be fine as soon as I get back to the war, where it's safe."

SHORT STORIES

God Knows What He's Doing

The announcer's voice was strong and resonant. "Give to Goodwill Industries," he said.

"Help the handicapped."

I limped to my transistor and switched it off.

My mother glanced up from her sewing. "Why did you do that?" she asked. "I wanted to hear the news."

"I don't like that commercial," I said.

My mother looked perplexed. "But why? They were just talking about helping the handicapped. Terry, you of all people—"

I stopped her before she could finish. "Look!" I blurted. "I know Goodwill does a lot of good, but I don't like to be reminded that I'm handicapped. I don't need them to help me. I just want to be left alone."

Mama sighed. "I've never seen you like this before, son. What's wrong?"

"Look at me!" I shouted, hobbling quickly toward her. "Look at how I walk. That's what's wrong with me. I can't walk." Suddenly, I started to cry. "I hate myself." I sobbed. "I wish I'd never been born."

Mama's face was sad. She spoke slowly. "Don't say that, Terry," she said firmly. "God has a place for you, or you wouldn't be here. He put you here to serve Him."

"Then why did He put me here with cerebral palsy?" I asked. "I could serve Him a lot better if I walked straight."

"I know it's hard," she answered, "but God knows what He's doing. He will never give you a burden you can't bear."

"I don't believe that," I retorted. "I'm not even sure I believe in God."

My mother was horrified. She was a devout Christian, and she had reared her children to be likewise. "Now you listen to me, Terry Taylor," she said. "You haven't been to church in three weeks, and I can't help that. You're too big for me to make you go anymore, but I can help what

you say, and I will not have such talk in my house. Understand me? I will not tolerate it."

"Then I won't stay in your house," I shouted. I grabbed my transistor and a basketball and stormed out the door. I raced awkwardly toward the ball court in the backyard. When I reached it, I turned the radio up loud and began to shoot free throws. Basketball and music were the two things I loved. They helped relieve my frustration.

I was born with cerebral palsy. I had what the doctors called a light case, and it affected me only from the waist down. From the waist up, I was perfectly normal, and my speech was completely unaffected. I know I was a lot luckier than most cerebral palsy victims. Through my childhood, I had considered myself quite fortunate. But now I was fourteen, and life was changing for me. My friends were beginning to date and do all kinds of cool things that I just couldn't do. I began to feel left out. I began to be self-conscious. I was frustrated and depressed. I tried to talk to Mom about it, and I prayed an awful lot, but it didn't seem to help. School was out, but the summer was no fun. I had never been so dejected in my life.

I pondered these things as I shot the basketball. That was the worst part about having cerebral palsy. I couldn't play ball. Everyone in my family was a ball player. My brother Sam was a sophomore forward at Ranger Junior College, and my brother Len had just made All-State guard at Lincoln High. If it hadn't been for my handicap, I would have been a good player too. I could outshoot either of my brothers, and at fourteen, I was already six feet tall. The knowledge that I would have been a good player only made things worse. I was really bitter about not playing.

I had shot for over an hour when a car drove in the yard. A tall, lanky young man got out. I didn't recognize him, but I heard Mother say, "Come in, Reverend," so I knew he must be our new preacher. He had only been in town two weeks, and since I'd been skipping church, I hadn't met him ye. But Mother had mentioned that he played basketball in college, and his athletic appearance seemed to bear this out. I was tempted to go meet him, but the Rolling Stones were singing loudly, and I was shooting well. I decided to stay where I was.

Suddenly I looked up, and he was standing under the goal. He rebounded my missed shot and

threw it back to me. "Hi, Terry," he said. "I'm Reverend Walker. Can we talk?" "I guess," I answered, shooting again.

He came right to the point. "Your mother says you wish you'd never been born."

"That's right," I said.

"God doesn't want you to feel that way," he said solemnly.

I replied quickly, "God doesn't want me to play basketball either."

"There's more to life than basketball," he stated.

"That's easy for you to say," I told him. "But you got to play."

"That's true," he admitted. "I did play, but I stopped when my eligibility was up. That's the whole point, Terry. Everyone stops sooner or later. Even the pros. There's only one way to stay involved in basketball all your life, and that's to coach it."

"So, what's that got to do with me?" I asked.

The reverend rubbed his chin thoughtfully. "Well," he said, "your mother says you know the game, and it's obvious that you're intelligent. If you study, there's no reason why you can't be a fine coach."

"But there's really no way to study," I argued. "You can't learn much just watching games. I need a coach to teach me things, and since I can't play, I'll never have a coach."

The reverend was silent for a moment. "Are you going to Lincoln High this year?" he asked.

"I guess," I said. "Both my brothers did."

"Why don't you go to Jefferson instead?"

"Well, I wouldn't mind," I said, "but why?"

He smiled. "Phil Lewis is the coach there. He and I went to college together. If I recommend you, he'll let you be manager. You can learn a lot from him."

"I'll think about it," I said.

"Fair enough. Say," he said coaxingly, "I'd like to see you in church Sunday."

"I'm not interested in church," I said.

He shrugged, palmed my ball in his ham-like hand, and then nonchalantly dunked it. My

admiration was visibly apparent. He laid a hand on my shoulder. "See you in church, okay?"

"I'll think about that too," I promised and walked into the house.

I went to church that Sunday, and I went to Jefferson High in the fall. Coach Lewis was everything the reverend said he was. I learned an awful lot from him.

During the four years I went to Jefferson, we won district three times. We lost in Bi-District twice but went to regional my senior year. We got to the regional finals and had a nine-point lead in the third quarter. But disaster struck- our best player came down with a rebound and twisted his ankle. With him gone, we fell apart and lost by six points. Later, we sat in the dressing room feeling as if the world had ended. Some of the boys were crying, but Coach Lewis was smiling. "Don't take it so hard, boys," he said philosophically. "I'm proud of our team this year. I know a lot of really good coaches who work all their lives and never get as far as we have."

"But you're not just a good coach," I told him. "You're the best coach in Texas, and you deserved to go to State."

He looked at me a long time before he spoke. "You can be a better coach than I am, Terry. If you work hard, maybe you'll be the one who gets to State."

"I'll get there," I said quietly. "I promise you that." Then under my breath, I uttered a short prayer, "God, please let me go to State someday."

The next fall, I entered college. Coach Lewis and Reverend Walker both worked to get me a scholarship. I was the manager, trainer, and general all-around flunky for the basketball team. The job was important not only because it paid for my schooling, but it also allowed me to learn more about basketball. When I graduated, I went back to Jefferson High as Coach Lewis's assistant. I stayed two years. Then I got a head job in Houston and began my quest for the thing all coaches dream of: a trip to the State tournament.

My quest ended three years later. My first two years in Houston, we had good teams but didn't play well in regional. The third season began poorly. We lost our first three games, and I felt we wouldn't win district, let alone regional. But for some reason, we started playing better. At first, we won by a little, and then we started beating people bad. When district play started, we still just had three losses, and when district was over, we had those same three losses. Our winning streak impressed people, but I wasn't optimistic until we won Bi-District by twenty. Then I conceded we had a chance.

I began regional weekend as a nervous coach, and I ended it by making reservations in Austin. We won our first game by sixteen and the finals by fourteen, but we could have won either by much more. We were simply better than our opponents.

The next week, we took a chartered bus to Austin. The kids were happy. They were laughing and talking, but not me. I was busy praying. "God," I said, "thank You for letting us go to State. You answered my prayer, and I'm grateful. But, God, one more thing. Since we're going anyway, could You let us win at least one game? I don't want to be greedy, but one lousy game couldn't hurt."

We won our first game by twelve points. It was just like regional. We were better than our opponents. When it was over, I gave thanks to God. Then as an afterthought, I added, "Since we're this close, why don't You let us win tomorrow? It might be a long time before I get back to

Austin. Please let me win it this time."

We won it, but it wasn't easy. Neither team was ever ahead by more than three, and the lead changed twenty-one times. We finally won by one in a double overtime.

The place was bedlam when it was over, but somehow Coach Lewis and Reverend Walker found me. "I told you you were a better coach than me," Coach Lewis cried jubilantly.

"I had good kids," I said simply, "and I had a lot of help from you two and from Somebody up there."

Reverend Walker grinned. "I'm glad to see you're finally giving Him a little credit," he said.

The bus ride home was a happy one. The boys listened to a radio, and I read over a lesson I was to teach for our adult Bible class. I figured God had given a lot to me, and I had better try to give a little back to Him. The radio music was loud. I was about to ask them to turn it down when a commercial came on. "Give to Goodwill Industries," the announcer said. "Help the handicapped."

His words brought back a flood of memories. I closed my eyes and could almost hear my mother's voice. "God knows what He's doing. He will never give you a burden that you can't bear."

You were right, Mama, I thought. *God did know what He was doing.*

I must have had a strange look on my face because when I opened my eyes, the boys were staring at me. Edward Logan, my best guard, put his head on my shoulder. "Being handicapped never slowed you down much, did it, Coach?" he asked.

"Well, it slowed me down," I answered, "but it didn't stop me." The radio announcer was still talking about Goodwill Industries. "Say, fellows," I said, "turn that up a little. I want to hear what that guy's saying."

Making God's Team

Phil smiled broadly when Coach Stone said he had made the team. "I wouldn't usually pick a sophomore," he continued, "but you've got ability, Archer. I think you can help us win."

Phil blushed under the praise. "Thanks, Coach," he said.

"Wait a second," Coach said. "We're working out Sunday too."

"But that's against league rules," Phil said. "I've read the rule book."

The coach laughed. "The rule says we can't have a formal workout. That simply means I can't be here to coach you. It doesn't say anything about y'all working out on your own." Phil nodded, but he wasn't sure he understood. The coach kept speaking. "You see, I'll type my instructions, and since Harper's the captain, I'll give them to him. You boys will come about one and leave around four. There's nothing illegal this way, but it sure gives us an edge on our opponents." He looked at Phil intently. "You don't mind working out extra, do you? We don't want anybody on this team who's lazy."

Phil stammered, "I don't mind. It's just that on Sunday I—" He stopped when he sensed the coach's disapproval.

"Go on," Coach Stone said. "What do you do on Sunday?"

"Nothing," Phil said, hurrying to leave. "Just forget it. Working out Sunday is okay with me."

But it wasn't okay, and he knew it. Phil's father was a devout Christian. He tried to keep all the Commandments, and he was especially particular about the Sabbath. The Archer family went to church Sunday morning and Sunday night. Most of their friends did too. What separated them from other Christians was that they tried to use the rest of Sunday for doing God's work as well. On Sunday afternoons, the family would go to the orphanage, the hospital, or the nursing homes, or sometimes they just did work for a neighbor who couldn't do it himself. The whole Sabbath was devoted to helping others. Mr. Archer called it "giving a little extra". Yet, he always claimed that he got more than he gave. Phil had been reared with this custom and he agreed completely with his father. He never finished a Sunday without feeling fulfilled. He helped others, but he was the greatest benefactor.

For the last several months, he had spent Sundays at a nursing home. All he really did was visit, but his youth and vitality seemed to give the aged new life. They were always sad when he left and glad when he returned. For many, he was their only visitor, and it gave him pleasure to curb their loneliness.

They would expect him Sunday. Yet, because of the workout, he would not be there. He knew they would be disappointed. He also knew that his father would be upset. He expected a severe dressing down. But Mr. Archer surprised him. When he heard the news, he replied calmly, "Well, Phil, I know what basketball means to you, and if you want to play, you can. This is one time I won't try to influence you. You'll have to make your own decision."

Phil felt a mixture of pleasure and disappointment. He was glad his father wasn't mad, but he had hoped he would tell him what to do. Now, whatever he decided, he had no one to blame but himself.

He spent the next night thinking and praying. The next morning, he went to see Coach Stone. He explained his decision and then said simply, "I want to play for you, but I guess it's a question of whether I want to make your team or God's."

The coach smiled. "I admire you, son. At least you have the courage of your convictions." He sighed wistfully. "I was religious when I was your age, but as I got older, I kind of got out of the habit."

"Maybe it's a habit you should pick up again," Phil said. "We'd be glad to see you in church."

"Thanks," the coach said, "but my religion is basketball now."

Phil went to the nursing home that Sunday. On his way home, he passed by the schoolhouse. It was late, but the guys were still playing. He was sure he recognized Coach Stone's car, but he decided he was wrong. That would make the workout illegal. The coach wasn't about to do anything that would keep him from winning. He looked at the gym. For a moment, he wished he was playing, but it didn't last long. He was sure he was doing the right thing.

When he arrived at school Monday, he was told to report to the coach. As soon as he saw him,

Coach Stone said, "Still want to play basketball?"

"Yeah," Phil said, "but I already explained why I can't."

"Yes, you can. I told the boys yesterday we're not having Sunday workouts anymore."

"Then that *was* your car. But why, Coach? I thought you said it helped you win."

"It does," Stone said, "but maybe I overemphasize winning. And maybe since the guys have

Sunday free, you could get them interested in the kind of work you've been doing."

"I could try," Phil said.

"Do you need any help at the nursing home?"

"Sure, but do you really think the guys would want to help?"

"I wasn't asking for them," said Stone. "I was volunteering myself."

"You mean you want to work at the nursing home?"

"Yes," said the coach, "and I'm going to start going to church too. You're not the only one who wants to make God's team."

The Dullness of Excitement

Jenny walked resignedly into the counselor's office. He smiled at her, and she tried to smile back. But it was more of a sneer. He could almost feel her contempt.

"Well, Jenny," he began, "they say you're giving trouble again. Is it true?"

Jenny frowned. "My grades are slipping, Mr. Parker," she admitted. "I don't know if that's exactly trouble. I don't know why everyone is so concerned."

Mr. Parker spoke sternly. "We're concerned because you have such potential. All your tests show that you should be an A student. Now, why don't you live up to those tests?"

"It's my weight," Jenny said.

The counselor looked at her closely. She was a tall girl with long, dark hair and straight white teeth. It was true she was overweight, but she was not unattractive. In fact, she had a vulnerable quality that made her downright pretty.

"How does your weight affect your grades?" he asked.

"I just worry about it, and I can't concentrate."

"Then why don't you diet and lose weight?"

"I crash diet all the time," she said. "It doesn't do any good."

"Well, if that's your trouble," said the counselor, "I know a doctor who can put you on a sensible weight-reducing program. Crash diets are dangerous, and they seldom work anyway."

Jenny smiled happily. "Will he really help me lose weight?" she asked.

"He'll help you, Jenny," Mr. Parker said. "But is your weight your real trouble?"

"The weight's the problem," Jenny declared. "It keeps me from concentrating. It keeps me... it keeps me from dating who I want to."

"Then you don't really have a weight problem." He chuckled. "You have a boyfriend problem, and you think losing weight will solve it."

"Scott's not my boyfriend," Jenny said. "He wouldn't go with me now. But once I lose weight, he'll change his mind."

"You mean Scott Miller? What about Phil Sharp?"

"Phil's a bore," she said. "The only thing about him that isn't dull is his last name."

"But you two had talked of getting married."

"We talked about it," she said, "but Phil wanted to wait. He said we couldn't marry until we finish college." She wrung her hands in anguish. "That's at least five years."

"That was a sensible decision," said Mr. Parker. "Most kids his age wouldn't have made it."

"That's the trouble," scoffed Jenny. "He's too sensible. Going with him is like having a third parent. He never wants to do anything exciting."

"So you broke up."

"Yes."

"And you think Scott will be more exciting than Phil?"

"I know he will," she said. "And he'll go with me, too, as soon as I lose this weight."

"You worry too much about the way you look," stated Mr. Parker. "Phil appreciated you for your mind. All your friends do. Why shouldn't Scott like you for the same reason?"

"I watch the guys in the hall," said Jenny. "When a girl goes by, they don't stare at her mind. Scott can go with any girl in school. If I want him to notice me, I'll have to look better than they do. Will you still call that doctor for me?"

"I'll call him," Parker promised. "But I think you should know that the way a person looks is not as important as what they have inside. And I think you should realize that a serious youth like Phil will sometimes amount to more than an exciting boy like Scott. I know that boy, Jenny.

He's a little wilder than he should be."

Jenny didn't seem to hear what the counselor said. Instead, she excused herself and left the office. She had a dreamy look on her face. It didn't take much to know that she was thinking of

Scott Miller. He was the cutest boy she had ever known.

Mr. Parker called the doctor. Then he went out of town and didn't see Jenny for six weeks. Upon his return, he met her in the hall. She had lost about fifteen pounds and was holding hands with Scott Miller. Mr. Parker was struck by her beauty, but something about her bothered him. In a few minutes, he knew that it was. The vulnerability he found so attractive was no longer there.

Two days later, she came into his office. There was no contempt on her face now.

"How's Scott?" he asked.

"I'm not going with him," she said. "I'm dating Phil again."

"What happened?"

"Well, it was like you said." She laughed. "Scott runs with a pretty wild crowd and he wanted me to be wild too. I tried it for a while, but it just wasn't fun. To be honest, excitement is duller than I thought it would be."

"So you went back to Phil?"

"Yeah," she said. "I don't know if it will get serious. We're both gonna go to college. Then if we still like each other, maybe we'll get married."

"That's sensible," said Mr. Parker.

"Isn't it though?" She laughed. "Oh, speaking of college, my grades are up. We've got finals in three weeks, and if I do well, I can probably qualify for a scholarship."

"I'm proud of you, Jenny."

"Thank you," she said. "I owe a lot of it to you."

With that, she left his office. But in a moment, she returned. "Say," she teased, "I know you don't think looks are important, but don't you think that losing weight helped my appearance?"

Mr. Parker looked at her thoughtfully. She was smiling, and he noticed that the vulnerable look had returned. "Yes, Jenny," he admitted, "you look very pretty."

A Chance to Measure Up

Gerald laced his tennis shoes quickly. It was only a few minutes until game time. He smiled to himself. He was only a sophomore, and sophomores seldom made the varsity at Lincoln. Yet, here he was. Not only was he on the varsity, but he was starting.

The event was practically unprecedented. In fact, it had happened only once before. That had been to his brother, Steve. Steve, too, had started as a sophomore. Thinking of his brother made Gerald sad. He wished Steve could be here now. But Steve wasn't here. He wasn't anywhere. Steve was dead.

Coach Wilson came into the dressing room. His face was bright with excitement. "Well, fellas," he said, grinning, "the season is about to begin." Then he grew solemn. "We always have a

pregame prayer," he said. "Gerald, since you're our center, would you care to lead us?"

Gerald felt himself stiffen. "I'm sorry, Coach," he said. "I can't."

Coach Wilson seemed perplexed, but he didn't reply. Instead, he called on Monk Jaggers. Monk was a senior guard. He was only five feet eight, but he was the best ball handler on the team. He was also very religious.

Gerald bowed his head, but he didn't listen to the prayer. He used the time to think about Steve. Steve was eight years older than Gerald, and at six feet seven, he was five inches taller. He had won nearly every honor imaginable, but it never went to his head. Even after he made All-American in college, he spent a lot of time with his brother, trying to make him a good ball player.

Steve had been drafted by the Indiana Pacers. As soon as he knew he was chosen, he called his parents. He said he wanted to talk with them before he signed. But Steve never talked with his parents. He never signed either. On his way home that night, a wheel came off his car. The car skidded and hit a tree. Steve was killed instantly. The ironic part was that he was only five miles from home.

Gerald had been fairly religious up until then. But after that day two years ago, he lost his faith in God. In truth, he had lost his faith in everything. He had even quit playing basketball.

He only came out this year because of Coach Wilson. Coach Wilson had played ball with Steve in college, and he convinced Gerald that Steve would want him to play. And now here he was in his first varsity game, and he was already the starting center.

The prayer ended, and the boys took the floor. Gerald was two inches shorter than the Jefferson center, but he had good spring, and he got the tip. A moment later, he took a pass from Monk and hit a ten-foot bank shot. He scurried downcourt in time to get the rebound. Then he switched back to offense, retrieved a missed shot, and stuck it back in for two. The game was only thirty seconds old, and Lincoln led four to nothing. Jefferson called time-out.

Coach Wilson was exultant. "You look great out there, Gerald," he said. "Keep it up."

Those early seconds were indicative of the way the whole game would be. Lincoln won it 63–42, and had Coach Wilson not substituted liberally, the beating would have been worse. Gerald finished with twenty points, twelve rebounds, and seven assists, and he had only played three quarters. He boarded the team bus feeling pleased with himself. A moment later, Monk Jaggers came and sat beside him. "You were really something," he said. "I didn't realize how good you were."

"Thanks," Gerald said. "I was lucky."

"Well, I just hope it lasts," Monk said. "Man, we could win State."

Like Steve, Gerald thought. His teams had won the State championship twice. "That'd be nice," Gerald said. "I'd like that."

The two boys rode in comfortable silence. Then Monk spoke. "Say Gerald, why wouldn't you lead the prayer tonight?"

"I don't go in for stuff like that," Gerald said.

"Well, why don't you come to church with me Sunday? You might find out it's not so bad."

"I went to church when I was little," Gerald conceded. "I used to like it." His face grew grim. "But that was a long time ago, and besides, it won't bring my brother back."

"It won't bring him back," Monk admitted, "but it might help you to accept things better. It might help you understand."

"I don't want to understand it," Gerald snapped. His tone softened. "Please, Monk, I don't want to talk about it."

The bus rolled on, but the silence was no longer comfortable. Gerald was anxious to get home. If the coach hadn't stopped him, he would have been the first one off the bus. "Can I speak to you a minute, Gerald?" Wilson asked.

Gerald was apprehensive, but there was nothing he could do. "Sure, Coach," he said.

When the others were gone, Wilson said, "You were good out there tonight. Steve would have been proud."

"I could never be as good as him," Gerald said.

"Maybe not," Wilson said. "But few people could. You're still a fine player."

"Thank you."

"Why wouldn't you pray tonight?"

"I just went through that with Monk. I guess it's because I don't believe in God."

Wilson seemed shocked. "But why?" he asked.

"Well," Gerald said, "if there is a God, why would he take somebody like Steve? I mean, he worked all his life to become a pro ball player, and just when he realized his dream, he was killed. Now tell me, why would a merciful God do that to him?" Gerald's voice was shaking, and

there were tears in his eyes. "Tell the answer to that, Coach," he said. "Tell me."

Wilson touched Gerald on the shoulder. "I can't answer that, son, except to say that the Lord moves in mysterious ways."

Gerald snorted. "You sound more like a preacher than a coach," he said cynically.

"In some ways, I am," Wilson said. "But if I am, do you know who's responsible?"

"No."

"Your brother Steve. He was converted his last semester at college, and he converted me."

"I don't believe you," Gerald said.

"Well, it's true, and it wasn't just me. He converted lots of people."

"But he never told me, and he never told Mom and Dad."

"He was going to tell all of you," Wilson said. "That's why he was coming home that night."

"That's not true. He just wanted to talk to us before he signed."

"But he wasn't going to sign, Gerald. That's what he wanted to talk about. He was going to

tell y'all that he wanted to skip pro ball. He was going on to school to be a preacher."

Gerald started to protest again, but suddenly he knew it was true. He slumped in a chair and put his head in his hands. Coach Wilson continued to speak. "I don't know why the Lord took him, Gerald, but I do know Steve wouldn't want you to go through life not believing in God. He'd want Christ to be your Savior too. You say you can't measure up to Steve as a player. Well, maybe you can't, but you can measure up to him as a Christian. All you have to do is give yourself to God."

Coach Wilson got off the bus. Gerald waited a moment before he followed. There were still many things he didn't understand.

When he reached the car, he was surprised to see Monk Jaggers.

"Man, y'all were in there a long time," he said. "What did Coach say?"

"He just told me some things about my brother," Gerald said. "It's got me a little mixed up, but then I've been mixed up a long time."

Monk cleared his throat. "I don't want to be pushy," he said, "but going to church might help you to understand a lot of things."

"That's a good idea," Gerald said. "Does the invitation to go with you still hold?"

"It sure does."

"Then I'll be there." Gerald was smiling. "You know what I said about being mixed up?" "Yeah."

"Well, I've got a feeling it's not going to last."

The Size of the Heart

Basketball season ended in March, but Monk Jaggers and I never stopped playing. We stood in my driveway engaging in a hard game of horse. The sun was high, yet the May breeze kept us cool. After a half hour, Monk had an H, and though I normally won, I had an R. Then I missed a ten-foot bank shot to give me an S. Monk got a quizzical look on his face and chided me.

"You're off today, Tucker. Have trouble with your girl last night?"

"As a matter of fact, I did," I said. "Only she's not my girl now. Barbie and I broke up."

Monk was just fixing to shoot a hook, but the news shocked him, so he held up his shot. I was glad he did. I never could follow his hook shot. He spun the ball on his finger and sank down by a tree. "What happened?" he asked.

"She wants to date Red Jenkins," I said.

Monk nodded. "I knew she liked him," he muttered. "I just thought she liked you better."

"She does like me better."

"Then why's she going with Red?"

I smiled. "You won't believe this, old buddy," I said. "She's dating him because he's taller."

Monk didn't answer right away. He was something of a philosopher, and like most of that breed, he usually thought before he talked. Finally, he said, "Didn't you tell her that height doesn't matter, Bill? I mean, it's fine on a ball court; in life though, it's the size of a person's heart that counts."

"I told her all that," I said. "She just wouldn't listen. Said right now she's very concerned with physical appearance, and Red was the best physical specimen around." I shrugged my shoulders. "What can I do?" I asked.

Monk was thoughtful again. "I don't know," he said. "I'm just glad Pudgy doesn't feel that way. I'd never get a date."

Pudgy was the nickname of Monk's girlfriend, Patricia Lane. She was a short girl with a pleasing personality and a tendency toward plumpness. Monk and I were the guards on our basketball team. He was five foot four, and I was five foot eight. Red was our center. He was six foot one. My lack of height had never bothered me in basketball. I made up for it with speed.

Speed didn't help to win Barbie though. From that day on, she belonged to Red.

When I perceived she would never be mine, I quit school and joined the marines. It was only a month until graduation, yet it seemed like the proper thing to do. A person with a broken heart is supposed to act foolish.

The marines were not for me. I could never get used to military discipline, and I spent more time in the brig than anywhere else. It wasn't all bad though. I did meet some girls who didn't mind a fellow being short. That's the funny thing about the marines, because when I got out, I wasn't short anymore. I went in at five feet eight and one hundred thirty pounds, and three years later, I stood six feet three and weighed two hundred and thirty pounds. I don't know what caused my growth. Maybe it was the exercise or just the change in climate. Whatever the cause, I turned into a pretty good physical specimen.

Naturally, I thought about Barbie a lot. I wondered how she would like me at my new height, but I didn't let myself get too excited. I figured she was already married to Red.

My first day back, I stood in my driveway and shot baskets. Suddenly a blue car pulled up. It was Barbie. She leaped out and hugged me. "My goodness, Billy," she said admiringly, "you've grown so much. You're beautiful."

I blushed under her glances, and then I noticed the ring on her finger. "How is Red?" I asked.

Barbie seemed puzzled. "Red? Oh, Red Jenkins. Why, I haven't seen him in weeks."

I pointed to her hand. "But your ring," I stammered. "Who is your husband?"

Again, Barbie looked puzzled. Then she smiled. "That's right," she said. "You didn't know.

Monk and I were married just last month."

"Monk!" I almost screamed. "Why, he is only five foot four."

Barbie got a self-righteous look on her face. "Billy," she said, "height is okay on a ball court.

In life though, it's the size of the heart that counts."

I didn't know what to say. I borrowed a trick from Monk and began to spin the ball on my finger. Finally, I asked, "Did Red ever marry?"

"Yeah," she said. "He and Pudgy Lane got the cutest little boy you ever saw. He's redheaded and as fat as a butterball."

I turned and drove toward the basket. I was so tall it was easy for me to dunk it. I slammed the ball through the hoop and grinned at Barbie. "Tell Monk to come play horse," I said. "I got one shot he'll never be able to follow."

The Dance

The school bus slid around the curve. Somehow it narrowly missed the truck. The bus driver wiped sweat from his forehead. His quick reflexes had averted a real tragedy. But he was still scared. The kids were nervous too. They were all talking at once. Some were even crying. Everyone was very upset.

Everyone—that is—but Alice Adams. She was reading a book when the excitement started and had never looked up. She was oblivious to the commotion around her.

Sharon Foster tapped her on the shoulder. "Didn't you see what happened? That truck was on the wrong side of the road. We nearly got killed."

Alice glanced up from the romance she was reading. "I didn't see it," she admitted. "The book is so good I just didn't notice."

Sharon shook her head. "I don't see how you read so many books," she said.

Alice put the book away. She was a little embarrassed to be so involved in a book. But she was eighteen and had never had a date. She found her only romance in reading. Alice knew Sharon wanted to talk, so she tried to oblige. "Do you have a date for the prom Friday?" she asked.

"I'll probably go with Phil," Sharon said. "He's not a prize, but he is faithful. What about you? Do you have a date?"

Alice laughed ruefully. "You know better than that," she said. "No one would go with me."

Sharon looked at her friend. Alice was a short girl with straight blond hair and a homely face. Yet her face was just the start of her problem. At five foot four, she weighed close to one hundred and eighty. She was terribly overweight. All the boys and many of the girls made fun of her. "Awful Alice" they called her. Alice had almost no friends. Sharon was the only one. "Don't give up," she said sympathetically. "Why, Lance Lane might call you."

Alice sighed. Lance Lane was the handsomest boy in school. She had helped him with his Algebra, and he was very kind to her. Most of the kids were rude to her just to be popular. But Lance was so popular that he could go against the crowd. He always treated her with warmth, and she had a terrible crush on him. She had spent hours wishing he would ask her for a date. It was her fondest dream.

Her dream was impossible, of course. Lance was going steady with Elaine Jefferson. Elaine was something of a snob, but she was very pretty. She was sitting at the front of the bus right now, and that made Alice nervous. She hoped Elaine hadn't heard her and Sharon talking.

That night, Alice finished her romance and thought about Lance Lane. She knew the kids at school made fun of her. She had heard them whisper, "Awful Alice," when they thought she wasn't listening. Their remarks hurt her deeply, and she figured quite accurately that their attitude would change if she went with Lance. Popularity, Alice knew, was a very fickle thing.

Alice had just gone to bed when the phone rang. "It's for you," her mother said, "and it's a boy." Alice could feel the excitement in her mother's voice. Mrs. Adams was an attractive woman who worried because her daughter didn't date.

Alice went quickly to the phone. "Alice, this is Lance," a high voice said. "Would you like to go to the prom?"

His voice sounded strange, but Alice was so happy she overlooked it. "I'd love to," she said.

"What time will you come over?"

"Seven thirty," he answered. "See you then. Goodbye."

Alice hung up the phone. She couldn't believe it. "Who was it?" her mother asked.

"It was Lance," she cried. "I'm going to the prom with Lance."

Alice was too excited to sleep. She called Sharon Foster and told her the news. Sharon was surprised but happy. "Wait 'til the kids hear about this." She laughed. "You'll be the envy of every girl in school. Can't you just see their faces?"

Alice giggled. "I won't be able to see their faces," she said. "I'm not going to school tomorrow. I've got to stay here and work on my prom dress."

"Well, I'll see them," Sharon said, "and I'll give you a full report." The girls hung up and

Alice went to bed. It was the happiest night of her life.

The next day, Sharon got to school early. She wanted to tell the girls about Alice and Lance. She was too late though. They already knew. "Did you hear about Alice?" Faye Pearson snickered. "Can you believe it?"

"Yeah, she told me," Sharon replied. "Why are you laughing?"

"Because it's a joke. Elaine knows Alice is crazy about Lance, so she got Randy Clark to pretend he was him and call her up. Come on, Sharon. You don't really think Lance would go with Awful Alice, do you?"

"I don't know," Sharon said, "but I don't think it's funny."

"Well, everyone else does." Faye giggled. "The whole school is laughing about it."

Sharon was very upset. Her first impulse was to find Lance Lane. But Lance wasn't at school either. He was editor of the annual and he had the whole day off to sell annual ads. Then she considered calling Alice. She couldn't do it though. She knew it would break her heart. *At least this way she'll have the whole day to dream about Lance*, she thought. *Sometimes a dream is better than nothing.*

When Sharon got to the dance that night, she looked for Lance. He didn't arrive until late, and when he did, Elaine wasn't with him. Sharon waited until he asked her to dance; then she asked, "Where's Elaine?"

Lance looked grim. "We had a fight," he admitted. "She decided not to come."

"May I ask what it was about?"

"It was about Alice," he said. "I don't know why Elaine did it, but I'm not dating a girl who can be that mean."

Sharon was thoughtful. "Lance," she asked, "do you like Alice?"

"Yes," he said. "She's a very sweet girl."

"Well, just this once, couldn't you go out with her? She doesn't know the call was a hoax.

She's home waiting for you right now."

"That's a good idea." He grinned. "That would show Elaine and everyone else." He glanced at his watch. "It's awfully late though. She's going to wonder why I didn't come sooner."

Sharon smiled. "Phil and I will go with you. You can say you're late because we had car trouble and you stopped to help us."

"Good idea," Lance said. "Let's go."

Everyone climbed in Lance's car. They were in high spirits. They knew Alice would be happy. When they reached the street where she lived, they knew something was wrong. Cars were parked everywhere, and people milled about. "That's a police car," Phil said, "and there's an ambulance." They jumped from the car and rushed inside. Mrs. Adams was sitting on the couch. Her face was pale, and her eyes were red from crying.

"Mrs. Adams," Sharon said, "what's happened? Why are all these people here? Where's

Alice?"

Mrs. Adams began to sob. "Alice is dead," she said. "She hung herself with the belt from her prom dress." Mrs. Adams stared at Lance. "She thought you weren't coming. She knew

everyone would laugh. I guess she couldn't stand to be ridiculed anymore."

No one spoke. Trancelike, Sharon walked to Alice's room and peeped in. She saw the prom dress lying on the bed. It was very pretty. Then she noticed it was covered with tiny scraps of paper. She moved closer, but it was a while before she knew what it meant. Finally though, she understood. It was the romance Alice had been reading on the bus. She had ripped it out, page by page, and torn it to shreds.

A Plea for True Pacifism

A few years ago, a friend of mine joined the pacifist movement. She was very high on peace and was certain that her organization would save the world. I have pacifist leanings myself, so I encouraged her. But I also told her, "If you were a true pacifist, you would never drive an automobile." My friend was shocked. She had just gotten a new XKE and was reluctant to give it up. But she admitted I had a point, and I do.

We have killed enough people on our highways in the last ten years to make the Civil War look like a minor skirmish, yet we keep on killing.

Before a recent holiday, I heard a disc jockey calmly announce, "Thirty-two people will die in Texas this weekend from traffic deaths." He said it casually, as if he were giving the weather. But if thirty-two people had died in a hurricane, we would have declared the place a national disaster area. If thirty-two people had died in one weekend from an illness, we would have sent the best medical help available. If a maniac had climbed a tower and shot thirty-two people, we would have been shocked and appalled. But we are blasé about traffic deaths. We simply shake our heads, say "tisk, tisk", and drive on.

Now we live in a country where communist plots abound. That is, if we just don't like it, we say it is part of a communist plot.

A lot of people called the Watts riot a communist plot. I don't think so. Watts was simply a bunch of Black people who wanted to be treated like human beings. The communists could have inspired it. But I doubt it. Humanity is not supposed to be a big thing with communists.

A lot of people called Watergate a communist plot. I wish it had been. I hate to think that America could have produced a man like Richard Nixon. I would like to believe he was influenced by evil forces outside our country. But I don't. I think he thought of it all by himself.

So you see, I don't think much of communist plots. But maybe, just maybe, there is one about now. I am speaking of the sale of citizens band radios.

The CB craze is sweeping the country. A CB, of course, is actually just a shortwave radio hooked up in a car. It allows drivers to communicate with one another, and in theory, there is nothing wrong with that.

What it does in practice, however, is let one driver tell another where the highway patrol is located. This means that a driver with CB can speed almost at will.

Now, it has already been proven that the frequency of accidents increases directly with the rate of speed. It has also been proven that the severity of an accident increases directly with the rate of speed. Yet we keep on telling one another to go faster. We keep on telling one another how to die.

Maybe the communists invented the CB. They know our recklessness with automobiles. Why should they drop bombs on us? Why not let us kill ourselves?

So, what should we do about the automobile? I think education is the first step. Teach people to drive slower. Teach them to drive defensively. Teach them not to kill themselves.

Then make laws that call for lower speed limits and have strict enforcement of these laws.

CBs, of course, should be declared illegal.

And lastly, I think we should begin to consider other modes of transportation. Ecologists have already called for this, and I think pacifists should too. Indeed, I think all sane people should.

Of course, many argue that we cannot give up the automobile. They say that our economy is based on it. I agree that it is. But to them I simply say life is more important than money.

My friend, incidentally, did not give up her XKE. She was killed in a car wreck three weeks ago.

The Roller Coaster

Tom had the stomachache again. He thought it was indigestion. His mother thought it was ulcers. I thought he was a hypochondriac. I didn't tell him though. You can't say that to your best friend.

The three of us had stood in line for an hour. We wanted to ride the roller coaster. Now we were almost to the front. In a couple of minutes, we would get our tickets. Suddenly, Tom turned.

"I can't ride this," he said. "It'll make my stomach worse."

Teena grinned ruefully. "Okay," she said. "Andy and I will ride it." She strode toward the ticket window, and I limped after her.

As I paid for the tickets, the man gave me an envious look. "Nice-looking girl you got there, bud." I was still blushing when we climbed on the coaster.

Teena grinned. "That man thought you were my boyfriend," she said. "Does that embarrass you?"

"No," I said. "I'm flattered because he thought that. I mean, who would think a girl like you could go for a guy like me?"

Teena spoke sternly. "A lot of girls could go for you, Andy. Your handicap has given you a complex." She giggled. "Don't tell Tom about this. He'll be jealous."

The ride started before I could reply. The roller coaster lurched wildly, and Teena took my hand. Throughout the ride, I pretended the ticket man was right. I pretended she was my girl. The way she squeezed my hand made the fantasy seem real. It was the best ride I ever had.

As we got off the roller coaster, an elderly man bumped into me. I nearly fell, but he caught me. When I regained my balance, he said, "I say, young man, are you a polio victim?"

"No," I replied, "just a victim."

The man was embarrassed. He stammered, "I'm sorry, son. I shouldn't have asked."

I was immediately sorry for my quick retort. "That's okay," I said. "Yes, sir, I've had polio since I was three."

"I'm sorry," he said again. Then he clapped me on the shoulder and left.

Teena sighed. "I can see why you're self-conscious," she said, "with everybody asking you about it all the time."

"He meant well," I said.

We began to look for Tom, but he was nowhere to be found. That suited me. I wanted to talk to Teena.

"Did you mean what you said a while ago?"

"About you going with girls? Of course I did."

"Well then, since I'm suddenly so irresistible, I may as well tell you something."

"What?"

"If I had my pick of all the girls I know, I'd choose you."

Teena looked worried. Her eyes were sad. "I know you like me, Andy," she said.

"I've known it for a long time."

"Then will you go with me?"

"I'm supposed to be going steady with Tom," she said, "if we ever find him again. And I do like him, even if he does get sick a lot."

I knew what she meant. Tom may have been a hypochondriac, but he was a nice one, and he was probably the handsomest guy in school.

"Besides," she added, "Tom's your best friend. If I said yes, could you really steal his girl?"

"I suppose not," I said. "I feel disloyal for even trying."

"You needn't feel disloyal," she said, "and you needn't feel rejected. Just try Darlene Ingram. She'll be glad to go with you." She smiled and kissed me tenderly. Except for my mother, my sister, and a couple of old maid aunts, I had never been kissed by a girl. It tasted warm and sweet, and it kind of took my breath away.

"We'd better find Tom," I said.

We found him coming out of a drugstore. He was buying Pepto-Bismol. His stomach was really upset.

About two weeks later, I got the nerve to ask Darlene for a date. I wasn't exactly cool about it. As I recall, it went something like this. "Are you—would you—would you like to do something sometime?"

"Are you asking me for a date?"

"Yeah."

"Do you want it for tonight, next week, or when?"

"To-tonight."

"Okay, I'd like to go. But if you want to get anywhere with girls, you should work on your technique."

"I haven't had much practice," I mumbled.

"That's okay," she said. "You'll learn."

When I told Teena about it, she smiled wistfully and said, "I told you so." The smile reminded me of the day she kissed me. I didn't stick around to talk.

I didn't tell Tom about Darlene. We had gone out three or four times before he knew. Finally, he said, "I hear you're dating Darlene."

"Yeah."

"You like her?"

"Yeah. She's a lot of fun."

"You know I nearly asked her out myself."

"When?"

"Right before Teena and I started going steady."

"Why didn't you?"

"Well, my stomach was bothering me then." He sighed. "I just never got around to it."

"Well, for once, I'm glad you were sick," I said. "'Cause she's a really neat girl."

Actually, I wasn't telling the whole truth. Oh, I did like Darlene, and she was nice.

Unfortunately, I kept comparing her to Teena, and the comparison didn't do her much good.

I had thought of Teena often since the roller coaster ride. Several times, I considered asking her out again. But each time, I remembered what she'd said about Tom, and I knew I couldn't do it. He was my best friend. I couldn't steal his girl.

I finally convinced myself I should just be content with Darlene. She wasn't Teena, but she was sure better than no girl at all. Oddly enough, just when I got content with her, I lost her. I called to say I'd come when I could. Only she wasn't there. Her mother said she'd gone with Tom.

My initial reaction was surprise. Tom was my friend. He wouldn't steal my girl. My next response was to call Teena. I wasn't going to fink on Tom. I just wondered if she knew. I had barely gotten out a hello when she said, "Did you know Tom and I broke up?"

"I kinda guessed it," I said. Then I had an inspiration. "Would you go with me now?"

"I'd love to," she said, "only I can't tonight. We have company."

"We'll go tomorrow then," I told her. "Maybe we can ride the roller coaster."

"I'd like that," she said.

We hung up and I went to bed early. But I didn't sleep long. Around midnight, the phone rang. It was Tom.

"I guess you know about me and Darlene?"

"Yeah."

"Listen Andy, you're my best friend, and I'm sorry. I just hope you're not mad."

I thought of the date I had with Teena and smiled. "I'm not mad, Tom. How's your stomach?"

"It's been bad today," he said. "Darlene thinks I ought to get it x-rayed."

"That's a good idea."

"Andy, are you sure we're still friends?"

I thought of the day Teena kissed me. Soon, I would taste her kiss again. "Tom," I said, "I promise you're the best friend I've got."

Cartwheels for Christ

Brenda was walking through the shopping mall when she noticed Reverend Wilson. He smiled broadly when he saw her. "Hi, Brenda," he called. "Say, that basketball game was really something last night."

"Yes, it was," Brenda said. "The guys did a fine job."

"But it wasn't just the players," he said. "You cheerleaders did a fine job too. Honestly,
Brenda, I've never seen you so excited."

"Well," she said, laughing, "it was an important game. I mean, we were playing Bi-District."

"I agree completely," the preacher said. "I'm an avid basketball fan, and I wanted to win as much as you did. But it got me to thinking. If people can get that excited at ball games, why can't they get excited about Jesus? Why can't they turn cartwheels for Christ?"

Brenda smiled nervously. "I don't know," she said. "It's just different at games. Church is just..." Suddenly she spied Mark Lane. Mark was the captain of the ball team and her boyfriend.

She was supposed to meet him here. She used his appearance as an excuse to leave her pastor.

"There's my date," she said. "I'll see you, Reverend."

"Yes, Brenda," he said. "See you in church."

Brenda rushed toward Mark. "Hi," he said. "Wasn't that your preacher?"

"Yes," she said. "He saw me cheerleading at the ball game last night, and he was asking why I couldn't turn cartwheels for Christ."

Mark laughed. "If we win Regional," he said, "I'll turn a few cartwheels myself. Christ or no
Christ."

Brenda frowned. "Oh, Mark! You're terrible."

"Oh, come on, Brenda," he said. "You know you feel the same way I do."

Brenda sighed. Mark was right. She went to church every Sunday. But she really had no feelings about God. She went only to please her parents. She knew they wouldn't let her cheerlead if she stopped. And she had to cheerlead to be near Mark. Actually, he was the only thing she cared about, and she lived with the constant fear that he didn't feel the same way.

Mark seemed to read her thoughts. He liked to keep her insecure. Grinning impishly, he said,

"When you start harping on God, I think I ought to drop you and start dating Elaine Lawson." Elaine was also a cheerleader. She wasn't going with anyone right now, and it was no secret that she had eyes for Mark. Brenda hated her. She knew Mark was teasing. But just the thought of losing him made her heart ache.

"But, Mark, you wouldn't?"

"I don't know," he said. "She sent me a note in history telling me what a great game I played last night."

"But I told you you played great too. I always tell you that."

Mark chuckled. "Calm down, Brenda," he said. "I'm not going with Elaine, yet. Besides," he said, touching her cheek, "you're prettier than she is."

The rest of the evening went fine. Mark could be terribly nice when he wanted to. Brenda forgot his teasing and had a great time. But on the way home, her insecurity returned. She pictured Mark with Elaine, and jealousy filled her until she was physically sick. She remembered what the preacher said about getting excited over Jesus, and for a moment she tried to pray. But it was no use. *I'll turn my cartwheels for Mark*, she thought passionately. *I'll do anything to keep him.*

After supper, her father read his nightly bible verse. He had a strong, resonant voice that Brenda loved to hear. But tonight she couldn't listen. Dimly, she was aware that he was reading something about putting the Lord first, but Mark kept entering her mind, and she couldn't concentrate on what he said. When he finished, her father said, "You didn't pay attention tonight, Brenda."

"I'm sorry, Dad. I was preoccupied."

"Is it Mark?" "Yes."

Her father was a kind man and spoke gently. "You're too involved with that boy, Brenda.

He's a little self-centered. I'm not sure he's the one for you."

"He's the only one for me," she cried defiantly.

"Okay," her father said, "only maybe you should pray about it."

Brenda went to her room, but she didn't pray, and when she did sleep, she dreamed of Mark and Elaine. "You're neurotic," she told herself. "He said he wasn't going with Elaine. Things will look better in the morning."

But they didn't, and as soon as the phone rang, she knew why. "Hi," Elaine said cheerily.

"Guess who came to my house last night?"

Brenda knew the answer. "Mark," she said mechanically.

"Yes." Elaine giggled. "I think we'll be seeing a lot of each other now."

"But he was with me all yesterday afternoon."

"I know," Elaine said, "but I think from now on your evenings will be free." Brenda was numb. "See you at cheerleader practice," Elaine said.

Brenda hung up and began to cry. She couldn't go to cheerleader practice. She couldn't even face going to school. *Oh, Mark*, she thought. *How can I live without you?* For a few minutes, she let herself sob. Then from somewhere in the back of her mind, she heard her father's strong voice urging her to put God first.

Impulsively, she fell to her knees. It was the first time she had ever really prayed, and when it was over, she knew she could face life. She could go to school, and yes, even to cheerleader practice. She could cheer the boys right on through Regional and maybe even through State- only this time her cheering would not be for Mark. This time, the cartwheels she turned would be for Christ. Smiling serenely, she picked up the phone and called Reverend Wilson. She wanted him to be the first to know.

Thou Shalt Not Date Seniors

Janice Tommie glanced around the study hall and stared despondently at her history grade. Anyone else would have been pleased with a ninety-five, but not Janice. She seldom made below a hundred.

Bobby Tate limped up to Janice and smiled. "What did you get on the quiz?" he asked. Janice and Bobby were locked in a tight battle for valedictorian. They had always been rivals. Janice knew Bobby had done well. Otherwise, he wouldn't have asked.

"Just a ninety-five," she told him.

"I got a hundred," he said proudly. Then with unaccustomed humility, he added, "It was tough though. I studied all day Sunday."

"I didn't study any Sunday," Janice said. "On Sunday, we can only read the bible."

"I know," Bobby said. "Looks like the Lord would let you have a little time off to study history, don't it?"

Janice didn't answer. She just stared at Bobby. He was a short, skinny kid with straight, even teeth and a nice smile. He had been born with a light case of cerebral palsy, which caused him to walk with a shuffling gait. The cerebral palsy had not affected his IQ though. He was one of the smartest kids in school, and because of his personality, one of the most popular.

What cerebral palsy had done, however, was make him cynical. He was basically kindhearted, but he seldom let it show. One of his greatest talents was to take an area someone was sensitive about and simply pick it to pieces. Janice had devoutly religious parents, and she was very sensitive about her religion. Bobby knew this, and he never missed an opportunity to tease her about it.

Janice was about to reply to Bobby when Johnny Baldwin came into the room. He was the school's best athlete and very sophisticated socially. Right now, he was talking about getting drunk the night before. Bobby didn't drink much, but he wanted to. And he listened attentively. Janice, on the other hand, didn't approve of drinking. She turned away and concentrated on her history paper.

Bobby knew Janice's feelings and seized his chance. "What's the matter, Janice?" he asked, loud enough for everyone to hear. "Are you against drinking?"

"Yes, I am."

"But, Janice," Bobby said, "doesn't it say in the bible that Jesus turned the water into wine?"

"Yes," she admitted.

"Well, if Jesus Christ did that," he said, "how can He be against us folks drinking a beer now and then?" Janice sighed warily. Bobby was not religious, but he knew the bible better than anyone she had ever met. And he had this fantastic ability to take the words out of context and twist them to fit his exact point. She knew it was useless to argue with him. She reached in her purse and took out a chocolate bar. It was two hours until lunch, and she was hungry.

Bobby saw the candy and grinned impishly. "Can I have part of that?" he asked. Janice shook her head.

"You had your break a while ago," she said. "You should have gotten something then."

Bobby's voice took on a somber tone. "I was hungry, and you fed me not," he said. "Isn't that a sin, Janice?" Everyone laughed. Janice smiled resignedly and broke the bar in two. She gave him half and he ate it in one gulp. "You'll get your reward in Heaven," he declared, sounding for all the world like a preacher in his pulpit.

Everyone was laughing when William Morris appeared at the door. He was the high school principal and as such was supposed to be keeping the study hall. But he was seldom there. Instead, he used the period to take care of other school business. The kids talked and did pretty much as they pleased.

Right now, sweat dripped from his bald head, so obviously he had been engaged in some activity. "I want you boys to come with me," he called. "If we're going to get the gym ready for the spring dance, we'll have to get a move on." All the boys left but Bobby. His physical handicap rendered him virtually useless in such an endeavor. So he chose to stay with the girls and pass his time reading. Strangely enough, though he never went to church, he was reading the bible. That was how he knew it so well.

Next week was spring vacation, and it was always accompanied by a big dance. The dance was the highlight of the year, so it was natural for the girls to start talking about it.

"Are you going with David England?" someone asked Janice.

"No," she said, "my parents don't want me to go with David since he's a senior, and even if

they would let me date him, they wouldn't let me go to a dance."

"Oh, come on, Janice," Linda Simpson said. "You're seventeen years old, and besides, dancing isn't exactly a sin, is it?"

Bobby had been reading casually, but now he piped up. "Of course it is," he said. "Haven't you even read in the bible where it says 'Thou shalt not dance'? It comes right before the passage that says, 'Thou shalt not date seniors.'" The girls began to giggle, and Janice's face turned red. Normally she could take Bobby's teasing, but not this time. She was crazy about David England, and she desperately wanted to go to the dance with him. She didn't like being teased about it. It hurt too much.

"Someday, Bobby Tate," she declared angrily, "you'll learn to stop making fun of people."

Bobby patted her gingerly on the shoulder. "Now, now, Janice," he said, "don't get mad. Remember old Job and have patience."

This final slur was too much for Janice. She rushed quickly out of the room. When she reached the end of the hall, she turned into the vacant teacher's lounge and began to cry. In a few minutes, she heard a shuffle in the hall. She knew it was Bobby's footsteps.

He stuck his head in the door and said with an embarrassed chuckle, "I'm sorry, Janice. I shouldn't have said all that."

"It's okay," she told him. "It's just that I want to go to the dance with David so badly."

"I know," he said, "and I hope you get to." There were a few seconds of embarrassed silence. Then Bobby said, "I won't be going to the dance either. I have to spend next week in camp."

"Camp?" she said. "In March? Where are you going?"

"Kerrville," he answered. "It's a camp for..." He hesitated and then spit out the words, "Crippled children."

Janice was silent. She knew Bobby hated being different. "I don't want to go," he continued, "but Mom is all for it. And the Lion's Club is sending me. If I don't go, it will hurt their feelings."

"Well, maybe it will help you," Janice said. "It might be just what you need."

"Yeah, who knows," Bobby replied mockingly. "The Lord moves in mysterious ways, His wonders to perform."

"Now there you go again," Janice said. "Can't you ever be serious?"

"I'm sorry," Bobby said, "and I really hope you can go to the dance."

Spring vacation ended and the kids returned to school. Most were glad to be back, but none would admit it. It wouldn't have been cool. Janice met Bobby in the hall the first morning. "How was your holiday?" he asked.

Janice smiled broadly. "It was just great. My parents and I had a long talk, and they still wouldn't let me go to the dance, but they did let me go out with David. He and I are dating regularly now."

Bobby sighed. "I'm happy for you," he said.

"What about you?" she asked. "How was your vacation?"

Now it was Bobby's turn to smile. "It was quite an experience," he said. "For the first time in my life, I realized there are people who are worse off than me. I'm not going to be cynical

anymore, Janice. I'm just going to be grateful for being as well off as I am."

Janice looked doubtful. "I hope you can change," she said. "But I'll have to see it to believe it."

"But you will see it." Bobby laughed. "You see, I went and talked to your preacher, and he wants me to tell my story at church next Sunday. He says the way I know the bible, I might be a preacher someday. He says all I have to do is use my knowledge in a positive way." Bobby's face was bright with pleasure. "Do you think I could be, Janice?"

"I sure do," she said. "David and I will be at church to hear you Sunday."

Suddenly Janice noticed the hall was empty. "We're going to be late for history," she said,

"and I bet we have a pop quiz."

"You're probably right," Bobby agreed. "Have you studied?"

"No," she answered. "I was out with David last night, and I didn't have time."

Bobby grinned cockily and smacked his lips. "I'm glad you didn't study," he said. "It'll sure be nice to beat you twice in a row."

How Far Does Friendship Go?

I had only been at Lincoln High for two weeks, but Sharon Ellis and I were already best friends. We ate lunch together, did homework together, and rode the school bus together. We had even double dated a couple of times. But today she tried to carry the relationship too far. "Hey, Mary," she said at lunch, "why don't you come to church with me Sunday?" Religion was one subject we had never gotten into and I was glad of it. It was one I didn't want to talk about.

"I can't, I said.

"But why?" she persisted.

I tried to think of an excuse, but I couldn't. So I just told the truth. "I can't go to church," I said flatly.

Sharon looked puzzled. "Mary, you know I work in the principal's office."

"Yes, I know."

"Well, I saw the registration cards you filled out when you first came."

"Yeah, so what?"

"Nothing—except under 'father's occupation,' you listed 'preacher.'"

"Yes, I did."

"But if your father's a preacher, how come you won't go to church?"

I could see why she was perplexed. "Well, actually," I said, "I filled out the card wrong. He was a preacher, but he's not anymore. He quit the church three years ago when Mom died."

"But if he doesn't preach, what does he do? How do you live?"

"He wrote a little book of poems. They're all about Mom and me and the way things were before—before Mom died. It didn't sell a lot, but he made some money, and he's still getting royalties. Other than that, he does odd jobs. He's a carpenter."

"Like Jesus," she said.

"Yes," I said. "Like Jesus."

"Why did he quit the church, Mary?" "That's personal," I said.

Sharon looked hurt. "I thought we were friends," she said.

164

"We are," I retorted. "But how far does friendship go? Doesn't it allow for any privacy?"

Sharon ducked her head. I immediately regretted my hasty words. "I'm sorry," I said. "I had no right to snap at you. My mother had cancer. She was thirty when she got it and

it took her three years to die." I started to cry. "It was a slow, painful death."

"I know," Sharon said.

For a moment, I wondered how she could possibly know. Then I went on. "From the first, the doctor told us to hold no hope," I said, "but my father was preaching then, and he never stopped believing God would save my mother. When He didn't, my dad went to pieces. I think he felt that God let him down."

"What about you?" she asked. "Do you think God let you down?"

"I don't know," I said. "But I love my father. He's the only thing I've got, and if he doesn't go to church, I won't either."

"I'd like to meet your father," Sharon said.

Now, Sharon and I were best friends, and as I said, we'd been doing homework together. But so far, we had always done it at her house. She had never been to mine. I had wanted to ask her over but felt I shouldn't. Now, for the first time, I could tell her why. "My father doesn't like company," I said. "Since Mom's death, he's almost a recluse."

"I'd still like to meet him," Sharon said. Her face had a strange expression. It was the same way she looked when she said, "I thought we were friends."

Again I thought, *How far does friendship go?* But this time I kept it to myself. "Okay, Sharon," I said reluctantly, "you can come tonight for dinner."

"I've got a better idea," she said. "You eat dinner with us. Then we can walk to your house together."

"Are you sure it's all right?"

"Sure," she said. "Jim and Nancy will be glad to have you." Jim and Nancy were Sharon's parents, but she always called them by their first names. I had eaten with them a lot lately, and I enjoyed it immensely. They were happy and vibrant people with an enthusiasm for life that was contagious. The gaiety in the Ellis house contrasted sharply with my somber home.

When we finished dinner, we walked to my house. I nervously introduced Sharon to Father, who smiled warmly and said, "Pleased to meet you, Sharon." When turning to me, he scratched his brown beard and said, "I'm glad you have a friend, Mary." This surprised me, but not as much as what he said next.

"I have to work in my workshop," he told Sharon. "Would you like to come out there and visit?"

Sharon glanced at the table where Father had eaten. "I'll help Mary with the dishes first. Then I'll come out." Father left, and Sharon exclaimed, "He's wonderful, Mary, and he's not only a carpenter like Jesus, he looks like Jesus."

"How do you know what Jesus looks like?" I asked.

"I don't," she admitted, "but we all have ideas, and to me, He looks like your father." I was pleased. It was quite a compliment. Sharon dried a couple of plates and then said, "Oh, Mary,

I just have to talk to him. Do you mind doing the dishes?"

"No," I said. "Go ahead."

Through the door, I could hear bits of their conversation. My father has a beautiful voice, and though I couldn't understand what he said, it was wonderful just to hear it. A couple of times, he even chuckled. It was the first time he had laughed since Mom died.

Finally, I finished the dishes and went out. Sharon was beaming, and Father quietly announced, "We'll be going to church with Sharon Sunday."

I was so surprised I couldn't speak. Sharon said she had to go, and trancelike, I walked her to the door. Then I managed to stammer, "How did you ever do that?"

"Well," Sharon said, "we just talked a while and then I told him about my own mother's death."

"Your mother?" I said. "But Nancy—"

"Nancy's my stepmother," Sharon said. "Jim married her four years ago. My own mother died when I was seven."

"Of cancer?" I asked.

"Yes," Sharon said. "I was younger than you, but I can still remember."

"That's why you said you knew it was painful."

"Yes."

"But your father," I said, "he seems so happy."

"My father was as broken up as your father," she said. "But instead of thinking God let him down, he seemed to draw strength from Him."

"And you told all this to my father?"

"Yes."

"And you convinced him."

"God doesn't want to lose a wonderful man like your father," Sharon said. "He wasn't hard to convince."

I thought of hearing my father talk and laugh.

"Thank you, Sharon," I said.

"We're friends," Sharon said. "I was glad to do it."

"How far does friendship go?" I said. "With you, it has no end."

Sharon smiled. "God wants it to be that way, Mary."

I smiled back at her. Then I turned and walked back to my father. He was smiling too.

The Premonition

It was the winter of 1950. The New England countryside was bleak and desolate.

What would later be called the Great Depression had begun. But the students here were not aware of it. Their school was fancy, and their homes were fancier. To them, poverty was simply a concept. It had nothing to do with reality.

The teacher was explaining diagramming to her pupils. They were a bright, eager class—far more alert than most children their age. She always enjoyed teaching them.

Suddenly, she noticed that one of the boys in the back wasn't listening. He was usually a fine scholar, and this perplexed her. "John," she called, "can you diagram this sentence?"

The boy scratched his tousled hair. "I'm sorry," he said. "I wasn't paying attention."

"Then what were you doing?"

"I was reading," he said. "It's a book about the Lincoln assassination."

"This is English class," she scolded. "We're not interested in Lincoln right now."

He smiled and diagrammed the sentence. As always, the quickness of his mind amazed her.

"Mrs. Carter," he asked earnestly, "why would anyone assassinate a president?"

"I don't know," she told him. "The country was involved in a lot of civil strife. I suppose some people lost their perspective."

He didn't answer, but his face looked troubled. She noticed that when she went back to the sentence, he started reading again. But she didn't correct him. He was obviously fascinated with the subject.

When class was over, he approached her desk. "Have you ever read this book?" he asked.

"Why, yes," she said. "I studied Lincoln quite a bit when I was younger. I'm glad he interests you."

"His death was a terrible thing," he said.

"Yes. Yes it was, but you needn't let it worry you. Nothing like that would ever happen again."

"How can you be sure?" he asked. "I mean, it's already happened twice since then."

"I know," she admitted, "but people are more civilized now. I think things like that are behind us."

He shook his head doubtfully. "I hope so," he said.

"Why, John," she said sharply, "you're just a born pessimist. Stop thinking about it now.

Don't be so morbid."

"Yes, ma'am," he said softly. He was smiling when he left the room.

After he had gone, she noticed he had left his book. She ran to catch him, but it was too late.

She picked up the book and read the inscription: "To John Fitzgerald Kennedy—from Dad." *It's a beautiful book*, she thought absently. *I'll give it back tomorrow.*

Pride

Mrs. Carter, our homeroom teacher, walked quickly to her desk. With one hand, she absently tugged at her hair. With the other, she opened her grade book. "Bobby Tate," she called, "are you eating today?"

I stopped writing my name on the desk and looked up. "Yes, ma'am," I said. "Charge please."

"Tarrance Strawberry,"

"Ch-Ch-Charge," Tarrance said. Tarrance always stuttered, and when he was nervous, he got worse. He was nervous today because he was copying my civics workbook. He was afraid Mrs.

Carter would catch him.

"Bud Wallace."

"Charge," Bud blurted. Bud was nervous too. He was supposed to get my workbook when

Tarrance finished. He knew if Tarrance got caught, he would never get it.

"Johnny Baldwin."

Johnny was backed up to the stove with his hands stuck in his pockets. His britches were so hot they smoldered. He rubbed his leg but kept standing there. "Charge," he said.

There was a commotion across the hall. Mrs. Carter cupped her ear to listen. "It's those sophomores," Linda Simpson said. "They're getting awful rowdy, Mrs. Carter."

"They certainly are," Mrs. Carter agreed. "Are you eating today, Linda?"

"No," Linda answered. "Mama said they're having goulash again." She wrinkled her nose. "I hate goulash." Linda's mother cooked in the lunchroom.

"She never eats," Richard Barker said.

"I know," I answered. "Wonder how she got so fat." Linda stuck her tongue out at me. I stuck my tongue out at her. We were locked in a tight battle for class salutatorian, and we didn't like each other.

"Richard Barker?" Mrs. Carter called.

Richard was scribbling obscene words on the bottom of his tennis shoe. "Here's a buck and a quarter," he told the teacher. "I'm paid up for the week."

"Janice Tommie?"

"Yes, ma'am, please," Janice answered. "I'm paid up through tomorrow." Janice was smart.

She was going to be class valedictorian. She was ugly, but she was okay.

"Clarence Kelly?"

"Clarence was absent yesterday," I said. "He went to see Mr. Norris to get an excuse." "I declare. I don't know why that boy misses so much," Mrs. Carter said.

And I don't know why your class roll isn't in alphabetical order, I thought. Mrs. Carter was nice, but she was scatterbrained. I thought a teacher should be organized.

Clarence Kelly came into the room. "Are you eating today, Clarence?" Mrs. Carter asked.

"Yes, ma'am. Charge," he said. He and Linda Simpson were cousins, but he liked her less than I did. "Here's my excuse for being absent yesterday," he said. Mrs. Carter signed the excuse without reading it. Clarence put it in his pocket. "Mrs. Carter, Mr. Norris said I should tell you that this is the last day for us to elect a student council representative. He said we should do it this morning."

Mrs. Carter tugged at her hair. She was flustered. She didn't like to get ultimatums from Mr. Norris, and she wasn't used to having Clarence Kelly talking to her. Clarence was the quietest boy in school. "Well, if you're going to have an election," she said, "I'll leave the room. This is a democracy. I don't want to influence anyone."

She walked toward the door, pulling her hair as she went. "Someday," I said, "she's going to pull her hair out." Everyone laughed.

Then Tarrance Strawberry leaned toward me. "Ta-Tate, are you sure number seven is tr-true?"

"Yes," I said. "In Texas, the lieutenant governor is more powerful than the governor."

Johnny Baldwin tapped me on the shoulder. "Tate, how would you like to be on the student council?"

"I don't know," I said. "I was on it when I was a freshman and we didn't do much."

"Well, I'm going to nominate you," Johnny said. I had tried to be casual, but inside I was glowing. My brother Johnny was in the eighth grade. Yesterday, the junior high had elected him their student council representative. He told my mother about it and she seemed very proud. I wanted her to be proud of me too.

Johnny walked to the front of the room. "I'm class president," he stated, as if anyone needed to be reminded, "and you are now at a meeting of the Hannibal junior class. This is just a little unorthodox, but I move we elect Bobby Tate to the student council by acclamation."

"I second the motion," said Richard Barker.

Johnny grinned. "All those in favor, raise your right hand."

Johnny Baldwin had come to Hannibal at the start of our freshman year. I was class president that year and student council representative, but after the kids got to know Johnny, I was never again elected to an important office. Johnny was class president our sophomore year. He was also class favorite and student council representative. This year, he had already been chosen class president and class favorite. And if this wasn't enough, Johnny was popular with the rest of the school too. He had been co-captain of the basketball team since his freshman year. Last year, he had been elected Mr. Hannibal High, and this year he had narrowly missed getting student body president. He had lost to a senior, and he was a cinch to win next year. I hadn't won anything important since my freshman year, but I wasn't jealous of Johnny. In fact, I liked him even better than the other kids did. Johnny just had charisma. He was good looking and he talked with a drawl. He kind of slurred his words together. Some people couldn't understand him, but it drove the girls wild. I spent hours trying to talk like him, and I got pretty good at it. Johnny was cool. He was my friend, and now he was getting me on the student council. I thought of how happy my mother would be.

Before anyone could raise their hand, Linda Simpson spoke up. "I have nothing against Bobby," she said, "but if this is a real democratic election, we should have at least two candidates."

Johnny smiled engagingly at Linda. She had a terrible crush on him and blushed every time he looked at her. He did not like her, but he knew his power over her. He looked at me and winked. I winked back. I knew she wouldn't nominate anyone else now. Then the bell rang. "We'll finish this in study hall next period," Johnny said. He rushed for the door. He always tried to practice basketball between classes. When he reached the door, he turned and threw a kiss to Linda Simpson. She turned as red as the cover of my loose-leaf notebook, but she was pleased.

Everyone left but Clarence Kelly, Bud Wallace, and me. We had homeroom and study hall in the same place, so I never left between classes. Clarence and Bud usually did though. I was surprised to see them there. "Aren't you two gonna get a coke?" I asked.

"We're not th-thirsty," Bud stammered. He stuttered almost as badly as Tarrance, and he was twice as dumb.

"I see," I said, though I didn't see.

"Do you want to be on the student council?" Clarence asked. Clarence almost never talked. Hearing him speak surprised me more than the question itself.

"I don't know," I said. "Not really." I was trying to appear indifferent. One could never openly seek an office in Hannibal High School. It wasn't cool.

"Well, if you really don't want it, nominate Baldwin," Clarence said.

"Yeah," Bud agreed, "nom-nominate Baldwin."

"Well, if you want Baldwin, why don't you nominate him?" I asked.

"I don't like to talk," Clarence said, "and Bud can't talk. At least not well. Will you do it for us?"

Slowly, I nodded my head yes. I was used to doing things for them. I had been doing their school work since first grade. But this was something I didn't want to do. I wanted to be on the student council myself. Clarence and Bud got up to leave. They had decided to get a coke after all.

I considered the situation. Johnny had nominated me and he would vote for me. Richard Baker probably would too. He always did what Johnny wanted. Tarrance Strawberry would probably vote for me too. He couldn't get through school without me. That made three votes. But both the girls would vote against me, and Clarence and Bud would make it four to three. I could tie if I voted for myself, but no one could openly vote for himself. I was licked, I decided. Johnny would win again. Mama would be disappointed.

In a few minutes, everyone came back. "Mr. Norris will be late," Johnny said. Mr. Norris was our superintendent. He was supposed to keep the study hall, but he almost never did. He usually spent the hour working on school business, and we normally did as we pleased. Occasionally, we got too loud, and Mrs. Carter would leave her English class across the hall and call us down.

Sometimes, like the sophomores, we got a little rowdy.

Johnny walked to the front of the room. "Let's finish the election," he said. Johnny's kiss had silenced Linda. She wasn't going to nominate anyone else. For a moment, no one spoke.

Clarence and Bud looked at me expectantly.

I cleared my throat. "Mr. President, I nominate ..." I hesitated, and then I had an inspiration. "I nominate Tarrance Strawberry."

"I second the motion," Richard Barker said. Richard liked to second motions. Bud Wallace had a surprised look on his face. He couldn't figure out why I had nominated Tarrance, but Clarence Kelly was seething. He knew I had betrayed him.

"All in favor of Tarrance, raise your hand," Johnny said. I was the only one who did. "Okay, all in favor of Bobby." Johnny and Richard quickly raised their hands. Then slowly the girls did too. *Even the girls voted for me*, I thought. *They know I'm the best choice of the two.* Clarence and Bud abstained. "Aren't you two going to vote?" Johnny asked. "Do you want to nominate someone else?"

For a moment, they were silent. Then Clarence said, "I guess we'll vote for Tate." They slowly raised their hands.

At that moment, William Norris bustled into the room. "Tate's our student council representative," Johnny told him.

"That's fine," he said, rubbing sweat from his bald head. "Johnny, you and Richard come with me. I'm having trouble with the intercom."

"That's not fair, Mr. Norris," Linda Simpson whined. "You always take the boys. We never get to go."

Norris sighed. "All right, you girls can go too." He looked at the rest of us. "Anyone else want to go?" he asked. I started to say yes, but Tarrance signaled he needed help with English. That suited me fine. I liked to diagram sentences. Besides, I didn't want to go anywhere with Linda Simpson. As they walked out the door, I saw Johnny Baldwin touch Linda Simpson's shoulder then squeeze it. He caught my eye and winked. I winked back. But I was a little unnerved. I was afraid he was beginning to like her.

Everyone left, and Tarrance got up to go too. "Where are you going?" I asked. "I thought you wanted me to do your English."

"I'm going to my locker," he said. "If we're going to diagram sentences, we'll need a ruler." He left. Clarence Kelly, Bud Wallace, and I were alone.

"Why did you nominate Tarrance?" asked Clarence.

I started to stammer. *I'm getting as bad as the rest of this class*, I thought. *I can't even talk*. Finally, I got control of my speech. "I thought it would do him good," I said. "Tarrance never wins anything. I thought it would help his confidence."

"That's a lie," Clarence said. "You did it because you wanted to win yourself."

"Yeah," Bud said. "You knew no-nobody would vote for old Strawberry."

I didn't answer them. There was nothing I could say. Clarence didn't have his civics, so I gave him my workbook. I felt guilty. After what I had done, it was the least I could do for him. When

Tarrance came back, I did his English. Then I did Bud's and Clarence's. But I still felt bad.

I had done their assignments for as long as I could remember. We had a simple system at Hannibal. The pupils who wanted to learn did their lessons and made As and Bs. The pupils who didn't want to learn copied their lessons and made As and Bs. I knew it was wrong to let them copy my work. But I felt it made them like me. More than anything else, I wanted to be popular.

That night, I told my mother I was on the student council just like Johnny. She was pleased to have her sons so honored. But her praise only made me feel worse.

Clarence Kelly was not at school the next day, but Bud Wallace gave me the cold shoulder. He warmed a little when I did his plane geometry, but he was still upset. All my teachers congratulated me, though. The basketball coach said I deserved it. My math teacher said I would serve well. Everyone was proud of me.

During homeroom the next day, we had our first student council meeting. My brother and I sat with the other representative and listened to Mr. Norris make a speech. He told us we were part of the decision-making process of the school. He compared us to the legislators who make decisions in the government. He said someday some of us might be in Congress. He said some of us might be senators. He was getting real stirred up. I am sure one of us would have made it to the White House if the door hadn't opened.

It was Clarence Kelly. He wanted an excuse slip for being absent the day before. My brother whispered to me, "Did you hear all the things Mr. Norris said? I wish Mom could have heard it. She would have been real proud." I glanced at Clarence. He glared at me. *Not if she knew how I got elected*, I thought.

Later in study hall, Clarence kept staring at me. I was trying to help Johnny with a feeding chart. He needed it for Vocational Agriculture II, and I knew how to make it, but I couldn't concentrate. Suddenly, Mrs. Carter stuck her head in the door. "Can I see you a minute, Bobby?" she asked. I knew we weren't being loud, and I couldn't decide why she wanted me. She handed me a mimeographed sheet of paper. The words were smeared, but I could make them out. It said, "Student council pictures will be taken for the annual next Tuesday. Students should dress accordingly."

Mrs. Carter smiled. "I'm proud of you, Bobby. I know your mother is too."

"Thank you," I said. I looked over at Clarence. His eyes were like fire. They burned a hole in my heart. Suddenly, I made a decision. "Mrs. Carter," I said, "where's Mr. Norris?"

"He's having bus trouble," she said. "At least I saw him going toward the bus shed."

"May I go see him?" I asked.

"Why, of course," she answered. Just then, we heard a thud across the hall. It sounded like someone hit the wall with an eraser. Mrs. Carter tugged at the hair. "Those children," she said. "I can't leave them for a minute."

She started back across the hall. I glanced at the back of her head. Her hair was getting thin. I smiled and started down the stairs to find Mr. Norris. I had decided to resign from the student council. I couldn't accept a position I had won unfairly, no matter how much I wanted it. I thought my mother would be proud of me for doing the honest thing- at least I hoped she would. When I reached the bottom of the stairs, I heard another loud noise. This time, it sounded as if someone had thrown a chair. For once in my life, I had to agree with Linda Simpson. *Those sophomores*, I thought, *are getting entirely too rowdy.*

The Professor

Merle Whitman glanced at the name over Professor Stone's door. It was the same plaque that had hung there years before. *I wonder if the professor will be the same*, Merle thought. *I wonder if he'll remember me.*

He knocked on the door and went in. The professor sat behind his desk. "Hello, Merle," he said, shaking hands. "How are you?"

"You remember me," Merle said.

"Of course I do. I can call all my old pupils by name. What are you doing now?"

"I'm writing," Merle said.

The professor didn't speak, but there was a skeptical look on his face. "You seem surprised," Merle said.

"I am. You see, I not only remember your name, I remember your compositions. You wrote

pretty well, but you never finished your work on time. I thought you hated writing."

"I did hate compositions," Merle admitted. "But it's different with short stories. I have to write them."

"Every would-be writer thinks he has to write," said the professor drily. "Most of them don't."

Merle shuffled his feet uneasily. The old man's attitude made him nervous. "Whatever happened to Phillip Wheeler?" the professor asked. "Now that's the boy I thought would write."

"He's tying steel in Dallas," Merle told him. "I think he makes good money."

"What good is money?" snorted the professor.

"Well, he's got three kids, and he's divorced. Alimony is high."

The professor got a resigned look on his face. "Alimony has ruined many good men," he said.

"You should know, Professor." Merle laughed. "How are Mrs. Stone and the children?"

"I never see her. I just mail the checks."

"What about the boys?"

"They're fine. The oldest is getting to be quite a poet. You can never tell though," he said sarcastically. "You never know who's going to write and who isn't."

Merle shuffled his feet again.

"How old are you, Merle?" the professor asked suddenly.

"Twenty-six, sir."

"Then don't you think it's time you started being realistic?"

"About what?"

"I mean, don't you think you ought to do something besides write for a living? You're being a little naive, son."

"You're not being fair," Merle said. "You haven't even seen my stories."

"No, but I saw your compositions, and the only good one you ever wrote for me was the one about that Elliot girl."

Merle was amazed at his memory. "Do you remember her, Professor?"

"Of course."

"Did you know I married her?"

"And I suppose you keep her barefoot and pregnant?"

"Well, we have twin boys."

"You'll be paying alimony yourself, young man."

"I doubt it," said Merle. "We're committed to each other."

"And you think it will last?"

"Yes."

"If you believe that," said the professor, "you're more naive than I thought."

Merle shuffled his feet.

"Have you sold any stories, Merle?"

"A few."

"But I read a lot, and I haven't seen your name. Is it a pen name?"

"No," Merle said. "It's my name. But, well sir, they're not exactly in the best magazines."

"Well, of course not," the professor said. "I should have realized they wouldn't be."

Merle got up to go.

The professor rose too. "Merle," he said, "why did you come here?"

"Well," Merle said, "you were my old English teacher. I thought you would want to know that I was writing."

"And did you expect encouragement?"

"Yes, sir. I, uh, guess so."

The professor smiled. "In that case," he said, sticking out his hand, "I wish you the best, and I think you'll succeed. Come visit again, son."

"Thank you," Merle said.

As he walked into the hall, he stared again at the nameplate above the door. *It hasn't changed*, he thought, *and the professor hasn't changed either.*

Uncle Bob

I smacked my lips as I set the table. We were having our usual Sunday dinner of fried chicken. We had had it every Sunday for as long as I could remember. But that didn't make me like it less. Nothing tasted better to me than chicken.

Mother smiled as she saw my anticipation. "Hungry, Susan?" she asked.

"Yes," I said. "I thought the pastor kept us a bit long today."

"It was a fine sermon," Mother said. "It doesn't hurt for lunch to be late." Then she added, "How was your new Sunday school teacher? Did you like him?"

"He was nice," I said, "and he really wants us to get involved at church. He said we should set a goal and witness to at least one new person each week."

Mother nodded approvingly. "We need to spread the Christian message," she said. "Oh, set another place, dear. Your Uncle Bob is coming to dinner."

"Uncle Bob," I said happily. "When did he get to town?"

"Last night," she said. "I was saving it for a surprise."

Uncle Bob was my father's younger brother. He was a professional basketball scout, and during the season, he traveled a lot. It was a real treat when we got to see him. Next to my parents, I thought he was the greatest person in the world.

My uncle Bob was an unusual man. From birth, he was affected by a light case of cerebral palsy. Because of this, he could not participate in sports. But he loved basketball and became an avid student of the game. He went to a basketball game every time he could, and when he wasn't watching basketball, he was reading about it. In time, he became so knowledgeable that coaches began asking his opinion on how to play opponents.

Finally, he decided to combine business with pleasure. He hired a couple of people to work for him and opened a professional scouting service. He would scout any team for anybody and charge a small fee. His scouting was completely objective, and the advice he gave was usually sound. In time, he had more games than he could handle. So he hired more workers and charged a larger fee. Now, after ten years, his firm was quite well known. He had turned his obsession for basketball into a lucrative business.

Of course, that was only the professional side of my uncle. I didn't really care how much money he made or what he did for a living. I only knew that he was good to me. We didn't see him often, but when we did, he always had a kind word or a funny story to tell me. He always treated me like I was special. So, naturally, I thought he was special too.

But as I stood there talking to Mother, I realized that in spite of my love for my uncle, I knew nothing about his religious beliefs. His visits were usually brief, and he always came on short notice. Religion had simply never come up.

Remembering my Sunday school teacher, I said, "Hey, Mom, when Uncle Bob gets here, I'll witness to him."

Mother seemed alarmed. "Well, I don't know, dear," she said. "That might not be a good idea."

"But why?" I asked. "You just said we need to spread the Christian message. Why can't I talk to Uncle Bob?

Mother sighed. "Your father and I talked to Uncle Bob when you were small. It was right

after we joined the church. He has some—well, he has some very anti-religious views."

I couldn't comprehend this. "But he is so good to everyone," I said. "He treats people like

Christ said to treat them. How can he be anti-religious?"

"I don't know," she said. "I agree with you. Bob is a very fine man. He treats everyone with a Christian attitude, but he is openly not a Christian. From what he told your father and me, I doubt he ever will be."

"Maybe I could talk to him," I said. "After all, you were just his sister- in-law. I'm his favorite niece."

Mother laughed. "I wish you luck," she said. "But I'm afraid you'll be disappointed."

Just then, the doorbell rang. "I'll get it," Dad called from the living room. But he didn't have to get it. Uncle Bob was in the kitchen before he finished speaking.

"Hello, Susan," he said, kissing me lightly.

"Hi," I said. "We don't usually see you this time of year."

He sniffed the air and winked at me. "Just needed some chicken," he said, "and I knew this was the best place to get it."

Uncle Bob loved chicken as much as I did.

"Well, Bob," my father said, "how's the basketball going?"

"You say basketball like it was a foreign word," Uncle Bob said. "Seems to me you were a pretty fair forward one time."

"That was a long time ago," Dad said.

"Oh, it wasn't so long," Uncle Bob said. "Do you know how good your dad was, Susan?"

I shook my head. "I knew he played," I said, "but I didn't know he was really good."

"He could have made All-American," Uncle Bob said. "Maybe even pro. But he decided to get married instead."

Mother laughed. "You've never forgiven me for that, have you?"

Uncle Bob smiled. "I didn't like it at the time," he said. "But it didn't turn out bad." He patted me on the head. "Here's one good result of it right here."

I blushed under his praise. "Let's eat," I said.

The dinner went quickly. My uncle entertained us with stories of his travels and predictions about who would be number one in college this year. As I listened to him speak, I thought, *How can this wonderful man not be a Christian?* I said a quick prayer. I knew I had to talk to him, and I hoped God would let me use the right words. When dinner was over, I nodded to Mom. She nodded at Dad, and though he didn't know of our discussion, he took his cue and followed her out.

Uncle Bob was busily attacking the last chicken wing. He looked up and laughed. "Where'd everybody go?" he asked.

"They stepped out," I said. "I want to talk to you."

"Oh," he said kindly, "go ahead."

I was excited, so I blurted, "I know you're anti-religious, so you probably won't approve, but I've been going to Sunday school, and I—"

"Wait a minute," Uncle Bob said. "I don't disapprove of Sunday school. If it gives you comfort, please go."

"Then why doesn't it give you comfort? I mean, Mom says you're not a Christian." My voice failed me, so I shrugged. "I don't understand it," I said weakly.

Uncle Bob sighed. "Look, Susan," he said gently, "it's true I'm not a Christian. But basically, I believe what you do. That is, do unto others as you would have them do unto you."

"Then why don't you go to church?" I said. "God is so wonderful, Uncle Bob. His goodness and His mercy are everywhere."

"That's just the point," he said. "You see, I don't believe God is merciful."

"But how can you not believe it?" I asked.

Uncle Bob looked at his legs. "Why would a merciful God give me cerebral palsy?" he said. "Why would He make me watch basketball when I wanted to play it? And why would He give me such a lonely life?"

"But you have a great life," I said. "You travel, and you make money, and you're well respected."

"Okay," he admitted. "In some ways, it's a good life. But it's not like what your father has here. It's not like having a family."

"But we're your family," I said. "We love you so much."

He shook his head. "You're a fantastic niece," he said. "Still, you're not like having a daughter. In spite of everything, something is missing in my life."

Again, I prayed to say the right words. "Uncle Bob," I said, "I don't know why you have cerebral palsy, and I don't know why you never found a wife and had a family. But I do know this. What's missing in your life is God. If you'll come to church with me, we'll find the

answers. If you seek *Him* first," I said boldly, "the other things will come to you."

Uncle Bob didn't speak. He simply walked from the room. Not knowing what else to do, I followed. Mother and Dad looked at me apprehensively.

Uncle Bob reached the door and then announced, "See you all next Sunday."

Dad was surprised. It was unprecedented for Uncle Bob to eat with us two weeks in a row. He simply never stayed around that long. "You mean you're going to eat with us again?" Dad asked.

"Well, I don't know about the eating," Uncle Bob said. "I'll see you next Sunday because I'm going to church with Susan." He laughed. "Of course, if the invitation to eat still holds, I might be persuaded."

"Of course," Mom said. "You can eat with us anytime."

"That's neat," Uncle Bob said. He smacked his lips and winked at me. "Nothing tastes better than chicken, does it, Susan?"

"No," I said. "No it doesn't." *And next Sunday*, I thought, *it'll taste better than it ever has before.*

CPSIA information can be obtained
at www.ICGtesting.com
Printed in the USA
LVHW042351040522
717841LV00049B/2013

9 781665 552448